WHAT GUNPOWDER PLOT WAS

View of the River Front of the House occupied by Whynniard

WHAT GUNPOWDER PLOT WAS

BY

SAMUEL RAWSON GARDINER, D.C.L., LL.D.

FELLOW OF MERTON COLLEGE, OXFORD

GREENWOOD PRESS, PUBLISHERS
NEW YORK

Originally published in 1897
by Longmans, Green, and Co.

First Greenwood Reprinting 1969

Library of Congress Catalogue Card Number 69-13902

SBN 8371-1806-9

PRINTED IN UNITED STATES OF AMERICA

CONTENTS

ILLUSTRATIONS

CHRONOLOGICAL NOTES

(*Political events in italics*)

1603. March 24.—*Accession of James I.*

June 17.—*James informs Rosny of his intention to remit the Recusancy fines.*

July 17.—*James assures a deputation of Catholics that the fines will be remitted.*

Aug. 20.—*Parry writes to announce the overtures of the Nuncio in Paris.*

1604. Feb. 22.—*Proclamation banishing priests.*

March.—Catesby imparts the design to Winter.

About the beginning of April.—Winter goes to Flanders.

Towards the end of April.—Winter returns with Fawkes.

Early in May.—The five conspirators take an oath, and then receive the sacrament.

May 24.—Agreement for a lease of part of Whynniard's block of houses.

June.—(Shortly before midsummer Keyes sworn in and intrusted with the charge of the powder at Lambeth).

July 7.—*The Royal consent given to a new Recusancy Act.*

Aug.—*Executions under the Recusancy Act.*

Sept. 5.—*Commission appointed to preside over the banishment of the priests.*

Sept. 14.—*The Council recommends that the Act shall not be put in force against lay Catholics.*

1604. Nov. 28.—*Fines required from thirteen Catholics rich enough to pay 20l. a month.*

About Dec.—Bates sworn.

About Dec. 11.—The five conspirators begin to dig the mine.

Before Christmas.—The diggers having reached the wall of the House of Lords, suspend their work.

1605. Jan.—The day cannot be fixed.—John Grant and Robert Winter sworn.

About Jan. 18.—Work resumed.

Jan.—Christopher Wright and Keyes brought to join in the work.

About Feb. 2.—Wall of House of Lords excavated half-way through.

Feb. 10.—*James orders that the Recusancy Act be fully executed.*

March, before Lady Day.—The conspirators begin to work a third time, but finding that the 'cellar' is to let, hire it, and having moved the powder into it, disperse.

Oct. 26.—Monteagle receives the letter.

27.—Ward informs Winter.

28.—Winter informs Catesby.

30.—Tresham returns to London.

31.—Winter summons Tresham.

Nov. 1.—Meeting of Tresham with Catesby and Winter.

2.—Winter meets Tresham at Lincoln's Inn.

3.—Meeting behind St. Clement's.

4.—Percy goes to Sion. Fawkes taken.

5.—Flight of the conspirators.

6.—Arrival at Huddington at 2 P.M.

7.—Arrival at Holbeche at 10 P.M.

8.—Capture at Holbeche.

WHAT GUNPOWDER PLOT WAS

CHAPTER I

HISTORICAL EVIDENCE

IN 'What was the Gunpowder Plot? The Traditional Story tested by Original Evidence,'[1] Father Gerard has set forth all the difficulties he found while sifting the accessible evidence, and has deduced from his examination a result which, though somewhat vague in itself, leaves upon his readers a very distinct impression that the celebrated conspiracy was mainly, if not altogether, a fiction devised by the Earl of Salisbury for the purpose of maintaining or strengthening his position in the government of the country under James I. Such, at least, is what I gather of Father Gerard's aim from a perusal of his book. Lest, however, I should in any way do him an injustice, I proceed to quote the summary placed by him at the conclusion of his argument:—

"The evidence available to us appears to establish

[1] London: Osgood, McIlvaine & Co., 1897.

principally two points: that the true history of the Gunpowder Plot is now known to no man, and that the history commonly received is certainly untrue.

"It is quite impossible to believe that the Government were not aware of the Plot long before they announced its discovery.

"It is difficult to believe that the proceedings of the conspirators were actually such as they are related to have been.

"It is unquestionable that the Government consistently falsified the story and the evidence as presented to the world, and that the points upon which they most insisted prove upon examination to be the most doubtful.

"There are grave reasons for the conclusion that the whole transaction was dexterously contrived for the purpose which in fact it opportunely served, by those who alone reaped benefit from it, and who showed themselves so unscrupulous in the manner of reaping."

No candid person, indeed, can feel surprise that any English Roman Catholic, especially a Roman Catholic priest, should feel anxious to wipe away the reproach which the plot has brought upon those who share his faith. Not merely were his spiritual predecessors subjected to a persecution borne with the noblest and least self-assertive constancy, simlpy in consequence of what is now known to all historical students to have been the entirely false charge that the plot emanated from, or was approved by the English Roman Catholics as a body, but this false belief prevailed so widely that it must have hindered, to no slight extent, the spread of that organisation which he regards as having been set forth by divine institution for the salvation of mankind. If Father Gerard has gone farther than this, and has attempted to show that even the handful of Catholics who took part in the plot were more sinned against than sinning, I, for one, am not inclined to condemn him very harshly, even if I am forced to repudiate alike his method and his conclusions.

Erroneous as I hold them, Father Gerard's conclusions at least call for patient inquiry. Up to this time critics have urged that parts at least of the public declarations of the Government were inconsistent with the evidence, and have even pointed to deliberate falsification. Father Gerard is, as far as I know, the first to go a step farther, and to argue that much of the evidence itself has been tampered with, on the ground that it is inconsistent with physical facts, so that things cannot possibly have happened as they are said to have happened in confessions attributed to the conspirators themselves. I can only speak for myself when I say that after reading much hostile criticism of Father Gerard's book—and I would especially refer to a most able review of it, so far as negative criticism can go, in the *Edinburgh Review* of January last—I did not feel that all difficulties had been removed, or that without further investigation I could safely maintain my former attitude towards the traditional story. It is, indeed, plain, as the *Edinburgh Review* has shown, that Father Gerard is unversed in the methods of historical inquiry which have guided recent scholars. Yet, for all that, he gives us hard nuts to crack; and, till they are cracked, the story of Gunpowder Plot cannot be allowed to settle down in peace.

It seems strange to find a writer so regardless of what is, in these days, considered the first canon of historical inquiry, that evidence worth having must be almost entirely the evidence of contemporaries who are in a position to know something about that which they assert. It is true that this canon must not be received pedantically. Tradition is worth something, at all events when it is not too far removed from its source. If a man whose character for truthfulness stands high, tells me that his father, also believed to be truthful, seriously informed him that he had seen a certain thing happen, I should be much more likely to believe that it was so than if a person, whom I knew to be untruthful, informed me that he had himself witnessed something at the present day. The historian is not bound, as the lawyer is, to reject hearsay evidence, because it is his business to ascertain the truth of individual assertions, whilst the lawyer has to think of the bearing of the evidence not merely on the case of the prisoner in the dock, but on an unrestricted number of possible prisoners, many of whom would be unjustly condemned if hearsay evidence were admitted. The historian is, however, bound to remember that evidence grows weaker with each link of the chain. The injunction, "Always leave a story better than you found it," is in accordance with the facts of human nature. Each reporter inevitably accentuates the side of the narrative which strikes his fancy, and drops some other part which interests him less. The rule laid down by the late Mr. Spedding, "When a thing is asserted as a fact, always ask who first reported it, and what means he had of knowing the truth," is an admirable corrective of loose traditional stories.

A further test has to be applied by each investigator for himself. When we have ascertained, as far as possible, on what evidence our knowledge of an alleged fact rests, we have to consider the inherent probability of the allegation. Is the statement about it in accordance with the general workings of human nature, or with the particular working of the nature of the persons to whom the action in question is ascribed? Father Gerard, for instance, lavishly employs this test. Again and again he tells us that such and such a statement is incredible, because, amongst other reasons, the people about whom it was made could not possibly have acted in the way ascribed to them. If I say in any of these cases that it appears to me probable that they did so act, it is merely one individual opinion against another. There is no mathematical certainty on either side. All we can respectively do is to set forth the reasons which incline us to one opinion or another, and leave the matter to others to judge as they see fit.

It will be necessary hereafter to deal at length with Father Gerard's attack upon the evidence, hitherto accepted as conclusive, of the facts of the plot. A short space may be allotted to the reasons for rejecting his preliminary argument, that it was the opinion of some contemporaries, and of some who lived in a later generation, that Salisbury contrived the plot in part, if not altogether. Does he realise how difficult it is to prove such a thing by any external evidence whatever? If hearsay evidence can be taken as an argument of probability, and, in some cases, of strong probability, it is where some one material fact is concerned. For instance, I am of opinion that it is very likely that the story of Cromwell's visit to the body of Charles I. on the night after the King's execution is true, though the evidence is only that Spence heard it from Pope, and Pope heard it, mediately or immediately, from Southampton, who, as is alleged, saw the scene with his own eyes. It is very different when we are concerned with evidence as to an intention necessarily kept secret, and only exhibited by overt acts in such form as tampering with documents, suggesting false explanation of evidence, and so forth. A rumour that Salisbury got up the plot is absolutely worthless; a rumour that he forged a particular instrument would be worth examining, because it might have proceeded from some one who had seen him do it.

For these reasons I must regard the whole of Father Gerard's third chapter on 'The Opinion of Contemporaries and Historians' as absolutely worthless. To ask Mr. Spedding's question, 'What means had they of knowing the truth?' is quite sufficient to condemn the so-called evidence. Professor Brewer, Lodge, and the author of the 'Annals of England,'[1] to whose statements Father Gerard looks for support, all wrote in the nineteenth century, and had no documents before them which we are unable to examine for ourselves. Nor is reliance to be placed on the statements of Father John Gerard, because though he is a contemporary witness he had no more knowledge of Salisbury's actions than any indifferent person, and had far less knowledge of the evidence than we ourselves possess. Bishop Talbot, again, we are told, asserted, in 1658, 'that Cecil was the contriver, or at least the fomenter, of [the plot],' because it 'was testified by one of his own domestic gentlemen, who advertised a certain Catholic, by name Master Buck, two months before, of a wicked design his master had against Catholics.'[2] Was Salisbury such an idiot as to inform his 'domestic gentleman' that he had made up his mind to invent Gunpowder Plot? What may reasonably be supposed to have happened—on the supposition that Master Buck reported the occurrence accurately—is that Salisbury had in familiar talk disclosed, what was no secret, his animosity against the Catholics, and his resolution to keep them down. Even the Puritan, Osborne, it seems, thought the discovery 'a neat device of the Treasurer's, he being very plentiful in such plots'; and the 'Anglican Bishop,' Goodman, writes, that 'the great

[1] *Gerard*, p. 48. [2] *Ib.* p. 51, note 2.

statesman had intelligence of all this, and because he would show his service to the State, he would first contrive and then discover a treason, and the more odious and hateful the treason were, his service would be the greater and the more acceptable.'[1] Father Grene again, in a letter written in 1666, says that Bishop Usher was divers times heard to say 'that if the papists knew what he knew, the blame of the Gunpowder Treason would not be with them.' "In like manner," adds Father Gerard, citing a book published in 1673. "we find it frequently asserted, on the authority of Lord Cobham and others, that King James himself, when he had time to realise the truth of the matter, was in the habit of speaking of the Fifth of November as 'Cecil's holiday.'"[2]

Lord Cobham (Richard Temple) was created a peer in 1669, so that the story is given on very second-hand evidence indeed. The allegation about Usher, even if true, is not to the point. We are all prepared now to say as much as Usher is represented as saying. The blame of the Gunpowder Treason does not lie on 'the papists.' It lies, at the most, on a small body of conspirators, and even in their case, the Government must bear a share of it, not because it invented or encouraged the plot, but because, by the reinforcement of the penal laws, it irritated ardent and excitable natures past endurance. If we had Usher's actual words before us we should know whether he meant more than this.

[1] *Goodman*, i. 102. [2] *Gerard*, pp. 46, 47.

At present we are entirely in the dark. As for the evidence of Goodman and Osborne, it proves no more than this, that there were rumours about to the effect that the plot was got up by Salisbury. Neither Osborne nor Goodman are exactly the authorities which stand high with a cautious inquirer, and they had neither of them any personal acquaintance with the facts. Yet we may fairly take it from them that rumours damaging to Salisbury were in circulation. Is it, however, necessary to prove this? It was inevitable that it should be so. Granted a Government which conducted its investigations in secret, and which when it saw fit to publish documents occasionally mutilated them to serve its own ends; granted, too, a system of trial which gave little scope to the prisoner to bring out the weakness of the prosecution, while it allowed evidence to be produced which might have been extracted under torture, and what was to be expected but that some people, in complete ignorance of the facts, should, whenever any very extraordinary charge was made, assert positively that the whole of the accusation had been invented by the Government for political purposes?

Once, indeed, Father Gerard proffers evidence which appears to bring the accusation which he has brought against Salisbury nearer home. He produces certain notes by an anonymous correspondent of Anthony Wood, preserved in Fulman's collection in the library of Corpus Christi College, Oxford.

"These remarkable notes, he tells us,[1] have been seen by Fulman, who inserted in the margin various questions and objections, to which the writer always supplied definite replies. In the following version this supplementary information is incorporated in the body of his statement, being distinguished by italics."[2]

The paper is as follows :—

"I should be glad to understand what your friend driveth at about the Fifth of November. It was without all peradventure a State plot. I have collected many pregnant circumstances concerning it.

"'Tis certain that the last Earl of Salisbury[3] confessed to William Lenthall it was his father's contrivance ; which Lenthall soon after told one Mr. Webb (*John Webb, Esq.*), a person of quality, and his kinsman, yet alive.

"Sir Henry Wotton says, 'twas usual with Cecil to create plots that he might have the honour of the discovery, or to such effect.

"The Lord Monteagle knew there was a letter to be sent to him before it came. (*Known by Edmund Church, Esq., his confidant.*)

"Sir Everard Digby's sons were both knighted soon after, and Sir Kenelm would often say it was a State design to disengage the king of his promise to the Pope and the King of Spain to indulge the Catholics if ever he came to be king here ; and somewhat to his[4] purpose was found in the Lord Wimbledon's papers after his death.

"Mr. Vowell, who was executed in the Rump time, did also affirm it so.

[1] *Gerard*, p. 159.

[2] I imagine that the notes in Roman type proceed from Wood's correspondent, and that Fulman's marginal questions are omitted; but Father Gerard is not clear on this.

[3] *I.e.*, the second Earl.

[4] ? this.

"Catesby's man (*George Bartlet*) on his death-bed confessed his master went to Salisbury House several nights before the discovery, and was always brought privately in at a back door."

Father Gerard, it is true, does not lay very great stress on this evidence; but neither does he subject it to the criticism to which it is reasonably open. What is to be thought, for instance, of the accuracy of a writer, who states that 'Sir Everard Digby's two sons were both knighted soon after,' when, as a matter of fact, the younger, Kenelm, was not knighted till 1623, and the elder, John, not till 1635? Neither Sir Kenelm's alleged talk, nor that of Wotton and Vowell, prove anything. On the statement about Catesby I shall have something to say later, and, as will be seen, I am quite ready to accept what is said about Monteagle. The most remarkable allegation in the paper is that relating to the second Earl of Salisbury. In the first place it may be noted that the story is produced long after the event. As the words imply that Lenthall was dead when they were written down, and as his death occurred in 1681, they relate to an event which occurred at least seventy-six years before the story took the shape in which it here reaches us. The second Earl of Salisbury, we are told, informed Lenthall that the plot was 'his father's contrivance,' and Lenthall told Webb. Are we quite sure that the story has not been altered in the telling? Such a very little change would be sufficient. If the second

Earl had only said, "People talked about my father having contrived the plot," there would be nothing to object to. If we cannot conceive either Lenthall or Webb being guilty of 'leaving the story better than they found it,'—though Wood, no doubt a prejudiced witness, says that Lenthall was 'the grand braggadocio and liar of the age in which he lived'[1]—our anonymous and erudite friend who perpetrated that little blunder about the knighthood of Sir Everard Digby's sons was quite capable of the feat. The strongest objection against the truth of the assertion, however, lies in its inherent improbability. Whatever else a statesman may communicate to his son, we may be sure that he does not confide to him such appalling guilt as this. A man who commits forgery, and thereby sends several innocent fellow creatures to torture and death, would surely not unburden his conscience to one of his own children. *Maxima debetur pueris reverentia.* Moreover the second Earl, who was only twenty-one years of age at his father's death, was much too dull to be an intellectual companion for him, and therefore the less likely to invite an unprecedented confidence.

It is not only on the reception of second-hand evidence that I find myself at variance with Father Gerard. I also object to his criticism as purely negative. He holds that the evidence in favour of the traditional story breaks down, but he has nothing to substitute for it. He has not made up his mind whether Salisbury

[1] *Athenæ*, iii. 902.

invented the whole plot or part of it, or merely knew of its existence, and allowed its development till a fitting time arrived for its suppression. Let me not be misunderstood. I do not for an instant complain of a historian for honestly avowing that he has not sufficient evidence to warrant a positive conclusion. What I do complain of is, that Father Gerard has not started any single hypothesis wherewith to test the evidence on which he relies, and has thereby neglected the most potent instrument of historical investigation. When a door-key is missing, the householder does not lose time in deploring the intricacy of the lock, he tries every key at his disposal to see whether it will fit the wards, and only sends for the locksmith when he finds that his own keys are useless. So it is with historical inquiry, at least in cases such as that of the Gunpowder Plot, where we have a considerable mass of evidence before us. Try, if need be, one hypothesis after another—Salisbury's guilt, his connivance, his innocence, or what you please. Apply them to the evidence, and when one fails to unlock the secret, try another. Only when all imaginable keys have failed have you a right to call the public to witness your avowal of incompetence to solve the riddle.

At all events, this is the course which I intend to pursue. My first hypothesis is that the traditional story is true—cellar, mine, the Monteagle letter and all. I cannot be content with merely negativing Father Gerard's inferences. I am certain that if this hypothesis of mine be false, it will be found to jar somewhere or another with established facts. In that case we must try another key. Of course there must be some ragged ends to the story—some details which must be left in doubt; but I shall ask my readers to watch narrowly whether the traditional story meets with any obstacles inconsistent with its substantial truth.

Before proceeding further, it will be well to remind my readers what the so-called traditional story is—or, rather, the story which has been told by writers who have in the present century availed themselves of the manuscript treasures now at our disposal, and which are for the most part in the Public Record Office. With this object, I cannot do better than borrow the succinct narrative of the Edinburgh Reviewer.[1]

Early in 1604, the three men, Robert Catesby, John Wright, and Thomas Winter, meeting in a house at Lambeth, resolved on a Powder Plot, though, of course, only in outline. By April they had added to their number Wright's brother-in-law, Thomas Percy, and Guy Fawkes, a Yorkshire man of respectable family, but actually a soldier of fortune, serving in the Spanish army in the Low Countries, who was specially brought over to England as a capable and resolute man. Later on they enlisted Wright's brother Christopher; Winter's brother Robert; Robert Keyes, and a few more; but all, with the exception of Thomas Bates, Catesby's servant, men of family, and for the most part of competent fortune, though Keyes is said to have been in straitened circumstances, and Catesby to have been impoverished by a heavy fine levied on him as a

[1] *Edin. Review*, January 1897, p. 192.

recusant.[1] Percy, a second cousin of the Earl of Northumberland, then captain of the Gentleman Pensioners, was admitted by him into that body in—it is said—an irregular manner, his relationship to the earl passing in lieu of the usual oath of fidelity. The position gave him some authority and license near the Court, and enabled him to hire a house, or part of a house, adjoining the House of Lords. From the cellar of this house they proposed to burrow under the House of Lords; to place there a large quantity of powder, and to blow up the whole when the King and his family were there assembled at the opening of Parliament. On December 11, 1604, they began to dig in the cellar, and after a fortnight's labour, having come to a thick wall, they left off work and separated for Christmas.

Early in January they began at the wall, which they found to be extremely hard, so that, after working for about two months,[2] they had not got more than half way through it. They then learned that a cellar actually under the House of Lords, and used as a coal cellar, was to be let; and as it was most suitable for their design, Percy hired it as though for his own use. The digging was stopped, and powder, to the amount of thirty-six barrels, was brought into the cellar, where it was stowed under heaps of coal or firewood, and so remained under the immediate care of Guy Fawkes,[3] till, on the night of November 4, 1605—the opening of Parliament being fixed for the next day—Sir Thomas Knyvet, with a party of men, was ordered to examine the cellar. He met Fawkes coming out of it, arrested him, and on a close search, found the powder, of

[1] This is a mistake. The fine of 3,000*l.* was imposed for his part in the Essex rebellion. (See *Jardine*, p. 31.)

[2] Off and on, a fortnight at the end of January and beginning of February, and then again probably for a very short time in March.

[3] Fawkes was absent part of the time.

which a mysterious warning had been conveyed to Lord Monteagle a few days before. On the news of this discovery the conspirators scattered, but by different roads rejoined each other in Warwickshire, whence, endeavouring to raise the country, they rode through Worcestershire, and were finally shot or taken prisoners at Holbeche in Staffordshire.

It is this story that I now propose to compare with the evidence. When any insuperable difficulties appear, it will be time to try another key. To reach the heart of the matter, let us put aside for the present all questions arising out of the alleged discovery of the plot through the letter received by Monteagle, and let us take it that Guy Fawkes has already been arrested, brought into the King's presence, and, on the morning of the 5th, is put through his first examination.

CHAPTER II

GUY FAWKES'S STORY

First of all, let us restrict ourselves to the story told by Guy Fawkes himself in the five[1] examinations to which he was subjected previously to his being put to the torture on November 9, and to the letters, proclamations, &c., issued by the Government during the four days commencing with the 5th. From these we learn, not only that Fawkes's account of the matter gradually developed, but that the knowledge of the Government also developed; a fact which fits in very well with the 'traditional story,' but which is hardly to be expected if the Government account of the affair was cut-and-dried from the first.

Fawkes's first examination took place on the 5th, and was conducted by Chief Justice Popham and Attorney-General Coke. It is true that only a copy has reached us, but it is a copy taken for Coke's use, as

[1] Mrs. Everett Green in her 'Calendar of Domestic State Papers,' adds a sixth (*Gunpowder Plot*, Book No. 50); but this is manifestly the deposition of November 17. It must be remembered that, when she produced this volume, Mrs. Everett Green was quite new to the work. She was deceived by an indorsement in the handwriting of the eighteenth century, assigning the document to the 8th.

is shown by the headings of each paragraph inserted in the margin in his own hand. It is therefore out of the question that Salisbury, if he had been so minded, would have been able to falsify it. Each page has the signature (in copy) of 'Jhon Jhonson,' the name by which Fawkes chose to be known.

The first part of the examination turns upon Fawkes's movements abroad, showing that the Government had already acquired information that he had been beyond sea. Fawkes showed no reluctance to speak of his own proceedings in the Low Countries, or to give the names of persons he had met there, and who were beyond the reach of his examiners. As to his movements after his return to England he was explicit enough so far as he was himself concerned, and also about Percy, whose servant he professed himself to be, and whose connection with the hiring of the house could not be concealed. Fawkes stated that after coming back to England he 'came to the lodging near the Upper House of Parliament,' and 'that Percy hired the house of Whynniard for 12*l.* rent, about a year and a half ago'; that his master, before his own going abroad, *i.e.*, before Easter, 1605, 'lay in the house about three or four times.' Further, he confessed 'that about Christmas last,' *i.e.*, Christmas, 1604, 'he brought in the night time gunpowder [to the cellar under the Upper House of Parliament.]' [1] Afterwards he told how he covered the powder with faggots, intending to

[1] The words between brackets are inserted in another hand.

blow up the King and the Lords; and, being pressed how he knew that the King would be in the House on the 5th, said he knew it only from general report and by the making ready of the King's barge; but he would have 'blown up the Upper House whensoever the King was there.' He further acknowledged that there was more than one person concerned in the conspiracy, and said he himself had promised not to reveal it, but denied that he had taken the sacrament on his promise. Where the promise was given he could not remember, except that it was in England. He refused to accuse his partners, saying that he himself had provided the powder, and defrayed the cost of his journey beyond sea, which was only undertaken 'to see the country, and to pass away the time.' When he went, he locked up the powder and took the key with him, and 'one Gibbons' wife, who dwells thereby, had the charge of the residue of the house.'

Such is that part of the story told by Fawkes which concerns us at present Of course there are discrepancies enough with other statements given later on, and Father Gerard makes the most of them. What he does not observe is that it is in the nature of the case that these discrepancies should exist. It is obvious that Fawkes, who, as subsequent experience shows, was no coward, had made up his mind to shield as far as possible his confederates, and to take the whole of the blame upon himself. He says, for instance, that Percy had only lain in the house for three or four days before Easter, 1605 ; a statement, as subsequent evidence proved, quite untrue ; he pretends not to know, except from rumour and the preparations of the barge, that the King was coming to the House of Lords on the 5th, a statement almost certainly untrue. In order not to criminate others, and especially any priest, he denies having taken the Sacrament on his promise, which is also untrue. What is more noticeable is that he makes no mention of the mine, about which so much was afterwards heard, evidently—so at least I read the evidence—because he did not wish to bring upon the stage those who had worked at it. If indeed the passage which I have placed in square brackets be accepted as evidence, Fawkes did more than keep silence upon the mine. He must have made a positive assertion, soon afterwards found to be untrue, that the cellar was hired several months before it really was.[1] This passage is, however, inserted in a different hand from the rest of the document. My own belief is that it gives a correct account of a statement made by the prisoner, but omitted by the clerk who made the copy for Coke, and inserted by some other person. Nobody that I can think of had the slightest interest in adding the words, whilst they are just what Fawkes might be expected to say if he wanted to lead his examiners off the scent. At all events, even if these words be left out of account, it must be admitted that Fawkes said nothing about the existence of a mine.

[1] It was not actually hired till about Lady Day, 1605.

Though Fawkes kept silence as to the mine, he did not keep silence on the desperate character of the work on which he had been engaged. "And," runs the record, "he confesseth that when the King had come to the Parliament House this present day, and the Upper House had been sitting, he meant to have fired the match and have fled for his own safety before the powder had taken fire, and confesseth that if he had not been apprehended this last night, he had blown up the Upper House, when the King, Lords, Bishops, and others had been there, and saith that he spake for [and provided] [1] those bars and crows of iron, some in one place, some in another, in London, lest it should be suspected, and saith that he had some of them in or about Gracious Street." [2]

After this it will little avail Father Gerard to produce arguments in support of the proposition that the story of the plot was contrived by the Government as long as this burning record is allowed to stand. Fawkes here clearly takes the whole terrible design, with the exception of the incident of the mine, on his own shoulders. He may have lied to save his friends; he certainly would not lie to save Salisbury.

So far, however, there is no proof that Salisbury was not long ago cognisant of the plot through one of the active conspirators. Yet, in that case, it might be supposed that the accounts that he gave of his discoveries

[1] Inserted in the same hand as that in which the words about the cellar were written. It will be observed that the insertion cannot serve any one's purpose.

[2] Gracechurch Street.

would be less dependent than they were on the partial revelations which came in day by day. There is, however, no hint of superior knowledge in the draft of a letter intended to be sent by Salisbury to Sir Thomas Parry, the English ambassador in Paris, and dated on November 6, the day after that on which Fawkes's first examination was taken :

Sir Thomas Parry, it hath pleased Almighty God, out of his singular goodness, to bring to light the most cruel and detestable practice against the person of his Majesty and the whole estate of this realm, that ever was conceived by the heart of man at any time or in any place whatsoever, by which practice there was intended not only the extirpation of the King's Majesty and his issue royal, but the whole subversion and downfal of this estate, the plot being to take away at an instant the King, Queen, Prince, Council, Nobility, Clergy, Judges, and the principal gentlemen of this realm, as they should have been yesterday altogether assembled at the Parliament House, in Westminster, the 5th of November, being Tuesday. The means how to have compassed so great an act, was not to be performed by strength of men or outward violence, for that might have be espied and prevented in time ; but by a secret conveying of a great quantity of gunpowder into a vault under the Upper House of Parliament, and so to have blown up all at a clap, if God out of his mercy and his just revenge against so great an abomination had not destined it to be discovered, though very miraculously even some twelve hours before the matter should have been put into execution. The person that was the principal undertaker of it, is one Johnson, a Yorkshire man, and servant to one Thomas Percy, a gentleman pensioner to his Majesty, and a near kinsman and a special confidant to the Earl of Northumberland. This

Percy had about a year and a half ago hired a part of Whynniard's house in the old palace, from whence he had access into this vault to lay his wood and coal, and as it seemeth now, taken this place of purpose to work some mischief in a fit time. He is a Papist by profession, and so is this his man Johnson, a desperate fellow, whom of late years he took into his service.

Into this vault Johnson had, at sundry times, very privately conveyed a great quantity of powder, and therewith filled two hogsheads and some thirty-two small barrels; all which he had cunningly covered with great store of billets and faggots, and on Tuesday [1] at midnight, as he was busy to prepare the things for execution was apprehended in the place itself with a false lantern, booted and spurred.[2]

There is not much knowledge here beyond what Salisbury had learnt from Fawkes's own statement with all its deceptions. Nor, if there had been any such knowledge, was it in any way revealed by the actions of the Government on the 5th or on the morning of the 6th. On the 5th a proclamation was issued for the apprehension of Percy alone.[3] On the same day Archbishop Bancroft forwarded to Salisbury a story, afterward known to be untrue, that Percy had been seen riding towards Croydon ; whilst Popham sent another untrue story that he had been seen riding towards Gravesend.[4] A letter from Waad, the Lieutenant of the Tower, of the

[1] A mistake for Monday if midnight is to be reckoned with the day preceding it.

[2] The remainder of the draft is occupied with the discovery of the plot.

[3] *Proclamation Book*, *R.O.*, p. 114.

[4] Bancroft to Salisbury, Nov. 5. Popham to Salisbury, Nov. 5.—*G. P. B.* Nos. 7, 9.

same date, revealed the truth that Percy had escaped northwards. Of course, Percy's house was searched for papers, but those discovered were of singularly little interest, and bore no relation to the plot.[1] An examination of a servant of Ambrose Rokewood, a Catholic gentleman afterwards known to have been involved in the plot, and of the landlady of the house in London in which Rokewood had been lodging, brought out the names of persons who had been in his company, some of whom were afterwards found to be amongst the conspirators; but there was nothing in these examinations to connect them with the plot, and there is no reason to suppose that they were prompted by anything more than a notion that it would generally be worth while to trace the movements of a noted Catholic gentleman. On the same day a letter from Chief Justice Popham shows that inquiries were being directed into the movements of other Catholics, and amongst them Christopher Wright, Keyes, and Winter; but the tone of the letter shows that Popham was merely acting upon general suspicion, and had no special information on which to work.[2] Up to the morning of November 6th, the action of Government was that of men feeling in the dark, so far as anything not revealed by Fawkes was concerned.

Commissioners were now appointed to conduct the investigation further. They were—Nottingham, Suffolk, Devonshire, Worcester, Northampton, Salisbury, Mar,

[1] Points and names of persons.—*S. P. Dom.* xvi. 9, 10.

[2] Popham to Salisbury, November 5. (*G. P. B.* No. 10.) The P.S. only is of the 6th.

and Popham, with Attorney-General Coke in attendance.[1] This was hardly a body of men who would knowingly cover an intrigue of Salisbury's:—Worcester is always understood to have been professedly a Catholic, Northampton was certainly one, though he attended the King's service, whilst Suffolk was friendly towards the Catholics;[2] and Nottingham, if he is no longer to be counted amongst them,[3] was at least not long afterwards a member of the party which favoured an alliance with Spain, and therefore a policy of toleration towards the Catholics. It is not the least of the objections to the view which Father Gerard has taken, that it would have been impossible for Salisbury to falsify examinations of prisoners without the connivance of these men.

Before five of these Commissioners—Nottingham, Suffolk, Devonshire, Northampton, and Salisbury—Fawkes was examined a second time on the forenoon of the 6th. In some way the Government had found out that Percy had had a new door made in the wall leading to the cellar, and they now drew from Fawkes an untrue statement that it was put in about the middle of Lent, that is to say, early in March 1605.[4] They had also discovered a pair of brewer's slings, by

[1] Narrative, *G. P. B.* No. 129.

[2] In a letter of advice sent to the Nuncio at Paris, on Sept. $\frac{10}{20}$, he is distinctly spoken of as a Catholic, as well as Worcester.—*Roman Transcripts*, *R.O.*

[3] On July $\frac{20}{30}$, 1605, Father Creswell writes to Paul V. that Nottingham showed him every civility 'that could be expected from one who does not profess our holy religion.'

[4] The 'cellar' was not really hired till a little before Easter, March 31.

which barrels were usually carried between two men, and they pressed Fawkes hard to say who was his partner in removing the barrels of gunpowder. He began by denying that he had had a partner at all, but finally answered that 'he cannot discover the party, but'—*i.e.* lest—'he shall bring him in question.' He also said that he had forgotten where he slept on Wednesday, Thursday or Friday in the week before his arrest.[1]

Upon this James himself intervened, submitting to the Commissioners a series of questions with the object of drawing out of the prisoner a true account of himself, and of his relations to Percy. A letter had been found on Fawkes when he was taken, directed not to Johnson, but to Fawkes, and this amongst other things had raised the King's suspicions. In his third examination, on the afternoon of the 6th, in the presence of Northampton, Devonshire, Nottingham, and Salisbury, Fawkes gave a good deal of information, more or less true, about himself; and, whilst still maintaining that his real name was Johnson, said that the letter, which was written by a Mrs. Bostock in Flanders, was addressed to him by another name 'because he called himself Fawkes,' that is to say, because he had acquired the name of Fawkes as an alias.

'If he will not otherwise confess,' the King had ended by saying, 'the gentler tortures are to be first used unto him, *et sic per gradus ad ima tenditur.*' To

[1] Second examination of Fawkes, November 6.—*G. P. B.* No. 16 A.

us living in the nineteenth century these words are simply horrible. As a Scotchman, however, James had long been familiar with the use of torture as an ordinary means of legal investigation, whilst even in England, though unknown to the law, that is to say, to the practice of the ordinary courts of justice, it had for some generations been used not infrequently by order of the Council to extract evidence from a recalcitrant witness, though, according to Bacon, not for the purpose of driving him to incriminate himself. Surely, if the use of torture was admissible at all, this was a case for its employment. The prisoner had informed the Government that he had been at the bottom of a plot of the most sanguinary kind, and had acknowledged by implication that there were fellow-conspirators whom he refused to name. If, indeed, Father Gerard's view of the case, that the Government, or at least Salisbury, had for some time known all about the conspiracy, nothing—not even the Gunpowder Plot itself—could be more atrocious than the infliction of torments on a fellow-creature to make him reveal a secret already in their possession. If, however, the evidence I have adduced be worth anything, this was by no means the case. What it shows is, that on the afternoon of the 6th all that the members of the Government were aware of was that an unknown number of conspirators were at large—they knew not where—and might at that very moment be appealing—they knew not with what effect—to Catholic landowners and their tenants, who were, without doubt, exasperated by the recent enforcement of the penal laws. We may, if we please, condemn the conduct of the Government which had brought the danger of a general Catholic rising within sight. We cannot deny that, at that particular moment, they had real cause of alarm. At all events, no immediate steps were taken to put this part of the King's orders in execution. Some little information, indeed, was coming in from other witnesses. In his first examination, on November 5, Fawkes had stated that in his absence he locked up the powder, and 'one Gibbons' wife who dwells thereby had the charge of the residue of the house.' An examination of her husband on the 5th, however, only elicited that he, being a porter, had with two others carried 3,000 billets into the vault.[1] On the 6th Ellen, the wife of Andrew Bright, stated that Percy's servant had, about the beginning of March, asked her to let the vault to his master, and that she had consented to abandon her tenancy of it if Mrs. Whynniard, from whom she held it, would consent. Mrs. Whynniard's consent having been obtained, Mrs. Bright, or rather Mrs. Skinner—she being a widow remarried subsequently to Andrew Bright[2]—

[1] Examination of Gibbons, November 5.—*S. P. Dom.* xvi. 14.

[2] "Mrs. Whynniard, however, tells us," writes Father Gerard (p. 73), "that the cellar was not to let, and that Bright had not the disposal of the lease, but one Skinner." What Mrs. Whynniard said was that the vault was 'let to Mr. Skinner of King Street; but that she and her husband were ready to consent if Mrs. Skinner's good will could be had.' 'Mr.' in the first writing of the name is evidently a slip of the clerk's, as Mrs. Whynniard goes on to speak of 'Mrs. Skinner then, and now the wife of Andrew Bright.'—*G. P. B.* No. 39.

received 2*l.* for giving up the premises. The important point in this evidence is that the date of March 1605, given as that on which Percy entered into possession of the cellar, showed that Fawkes's statement that he had brought powder into the cellar at Christmas 1604 could not possibly be true. On the 7th, Mrs. Whynniard confirmed Mrs. Bright's statement, and also stated that, a year earlier, in March 1604, 'Mr. Percy began to labour very earnestly with this examinate and her husband to have the lodging by the Parliament House, which one Mr. Henry Ferris, of Warwickshire, had long held before, and having obtained the said Mr. Ferris's good will to part from it after long suit by himself and great entreaty of Mr. Carleton, Mr. Epsley,[1] and other gentlemen belonging to the Earl of Northumberland, affirming him to be a very honest gentleman, and that they could not have a better tenant, her husband and she were contented to let him have the said lodging at the same rent Mr. Ferris paid for it.'[2] Mrs. Whynniard had plainly never heard of the mine; and

[1] Probably 'Hippesley.'

[2] Father Gerard, (p. 91, note 5) accepts Goodman's assertion that it was said that Whynniard 'as soon as ever he heard of the news what Percy intended, he instantly fell into a fright and died: so that it could not be certainly known who procured him the house, or by whose means.' That Whynniard was alive on the 7th is proved by the fact that Susan Whynniard is styled his wife and not his widow at the head of this examination. As he was himself not questioned it may be inferred that he was seriously ill at the time. That his illness was caused by fright is probably pure gossip. Mrs. Bright, when examined (*G.P.B.* No. 24) speaks of Mrs. Whynniard as agreeing to change the tenancy of the cellar, which looks as if the husband had been ill and inaccessible at least six months before his death.

that the Government was in equal ignorance is shown by the endorsement on the agreement of Ferris, or rather Ferrers, to make over his tenancy to Percy. 'The bargain between Ferris and Percy for the bloody cellar, found in Winter's lodging.' Winter's name had been under consideration for some little time, and doubtless the discovery of this paper was made on, or more probably before, the 7th. The Government, having as yet nothing but Fawkes's evidence to go upon, connected the hiring of the house with the hiring of the cellar, and at least showed no signs of suspecting anything more.

On the same day, the 7th, something was definitely heard of the proceedings of the other plotters, who had either gathered at Dunchurch for the hunting-match, or had fled from London to join them, and a proclamation was issued for the arrest of Percy, Catesby, Rokewood, Thomas Winter, Edward[1] Grant, John and Christopher Wright, and Catesby's servant, Robert Ashfield. They were charged with assembling in troops in the counties of Warwick and Worcester, breaking into stables and seizing horses.[2] Fawkes, too, was on that day subjected to a fourth examination.[3] Not very much that was new was extracted from him. He acknowledged that his real name was Guy Fawkes, that—which he had denied before—he had received the Sacrament not to discover any of the conspirators, and also that there had been at first five persons privy to the

[1] Properly 'John.'

[2] *S. P. Dom.* xvi. 20.

[3] *G. P. B.* No. 37. Witnessed by Northampton and Popham only.

plot, and afterwards five or six more 'were generally acquainted that an action was to be performed for the Catholic cause, and saith that he doth not know that they were acquainted with the whole conspiracy.' Being asked whether Catesby, the two Wrights, Winter, or Tresham were privy, he refused to accuse any one.

The increase of the information received by the Government left its trace on Salisbury's correspondence. Whether the letter to Parry, from which a quotation has already been given, was sent away on the 6th, is unknown ; but it was copied and completed, with sundry alterations, for Cornwallis and Edmondes, the ambassadors at Madrid and Brussels, and signed by Salisbury on the 7th, though it was kept back and sent off with two postscripts on the 9th, and it is likely enough that the letter to Parry was treated in the same way. One of the alterations concerns Fawkes's admission that he had taken the Sacrament as well as an oath to keep the secret. What is of greater significance is, that there is absolutely no mention of a mine in the letter. If it had really been written on the 9th, this silence would have gone far to justify Father Gerard's suspicions, as the existence of the mine was certainly known to the Government at that date. On the 7th the Government knew nothing of it.[1]

[1] The letter to Cornwallis, printed in Winwood's *Memorials*, ii. 170, is dated Nov. 9, as it is in Cott. MSS. Vesp. cix. fol. 240, from which it is printed. That volume, however, is merely a letter book. The letter to Edmondes, on the other hand, in the Stowe MSS. 168, fol. 213, is the original, with Salisbury's autograph signature, and its date has clearly been altered from 7 to 9.

That Fawkes had already been threatened with torture is known,[1] and it may easily be imagined that the threats had been redoubled after this last unsatisfactory acknowledgment. On the morning of the 8th, however, Waad, who was employed to worm out his secrets, reported that little was to be expected. "I find this fellow," he wrote, "who this day is in a most stubborn and perverse humour, as dogged as if he were possessed. Yesternight I had persuaded him to set down a clear narration of all his wicked plots from the first entering to the same, to the end they pretended, with the discourses and projects that were thought upon amongst them, which he undertook [to do] and craved time this night to bethink him the better; but this morning he hath changed his mind and is [so] sullen and obstinate as there is no dealing with him."[2]

The sight of the examiners, together with the sight of the rack,[3] changed Fawkes's mind to some extent. He was resolved that nothing but actual torture should wring from him the names of his fellow plotters, who so far as was known in London were still at large.[4] He prepared himself, however, to reveal the secrets of the plot so far as was consistent with the con-

[1] Waad to Salisbury, Nov. 7.—Hatfield MSS.

[2] Waad to Salisbury, Nov. 8.—*G. P. B.* No. 48 B.

[3] In 'The King's Book' it is stated that Fawkes was shown the rack, but never racked. Probably the torture used on the 9th was that of the manacles, or hanging up by the wrists or thumbs.

[4] The principal ones were either killed or taken at Holbeche on that very day.

cealment of the names of those concerned in it. His fifth examination on the 8th, the last before the one taken under torture on the 9th, gives to the inquirer into the reality of the plot all that he wants to know.'

"He confesseth," so the tale begins, "that a practice was first broken unto him against his Majesty for the Catholic cause, and not invented or propounded by himself, and this was first propounded unto him about Easter last was twelvemonth, beyond the seas in the Low Countries, by an English layman,[1] and that Englishman came over with him in his company, into England, and they two and three more [2] were the first five mentioned in the former examination. And they five resolving to do somewhat for the Catholic cause (a vow being first taken by all of them for secrecy), one of the other three [3] propounded to perform it with powder, and resolved that the place should be (where this action should be performed and justice done) in or near the place of the sitting of the Parliament, wherein Religion had been unjustly suppressed. This being resolved, the manner of it was as followeth :—

"First they hired the house at Westminster, of one Ferres, and having his house they sought then [4] to make a mine under the Upper House of Parliament, and they began to make the mine in or about the 11 of December, and they five first entered into the works, and soone after took an other [5] to [6] them, having first sworn him and taken

[1] Thomas Winter.

[2] Catesby, Percy, and John Wright.

[3] *I.e.* Catesby. In a copy forwarded to Edmondes by Salisbury (Stowe MSS. 168, fol. 223) the copyist had originally written 'three or four more,' which is altered to 'three.'

[4] 'Then,' omitted in the Stowe copy.

[5] Christopher Wright. [6] 'Unto,' in the Stowe copy.

the sacrament for secrecy; and when they came to the wall (that was about three yards thick) and found it a matter of great difficulty, they took to them an other in like manner, with oath and sacrament as aforesaid;[1] all which seven were gentlemen of name and blood, and not any[2] was employed in or about this action (no, not so much as in digging and mining) that was not a gentleman. And having wrought to the wall before Christmas, they ceased until after the holidays, and the day before Christmas (having a mass of earth that came out of the mine), they carried it into the garden of the said house, and after Christmas they wrought the wall till Candlemas, and wrought the wall half through; and saith that all the time while the other[3] wrought, he stood as sentinel, to descry any man that came near, and when any man came near to the place upon warning given by him, they ceased until they had notice to proceed from him, and sayeth that they seven all lay in the house, and had shot and powder, and they all resolved to die in that place, before they yielded or were taken.

"And, as they were working, they heard a rushing in the cellar, which grew by one[4] Bright's selling of his coals,[5] whereupon this examinant, fearing they had been discovered, went into the cellar, and viewed the cellar[6] and perceiving the commodity thereof for their purpose, and understanding how it would be letten,[7] his master, Mr. Percy, hired the cellar for a year for 4*l.* rent; and con-

[1] Robert Winter. The question whether Keyes worked at this time will be discussed later on.

[2] 'Any man,' in the Stowe copy. [3] 'Others,' in the Stowe copy.

[4] 'One' is inserted above the line.

[5] This is an obvious mistake, as the widow Skinner was not at this time married to Bright, but one just as likely to be made by Fawkes himself as by his examiners.

[6] 'Viewed it,' in the Stowe copy. [7] 'Taken,' in Stowe copy.

fesseth that after Christmas twenty barrels of powder were brought by themselves to a house, which they had on the Bankside in hampers, and from that house removed[1] the powder to the said house near the Upper House of Parliament; and presently, upon hiring the cellar they themselves removed the powder into the cellar, and covered the same with fagots which they had before laid into the cellar.

"After, about Easter, he went into the Low Countries (as he before hath declared in his former examination) and that the true purpose of his going over was, lest, being a dangerous man, he should be known and suspected, and in the mean time he left the key of the cellar with Mr. Percy, who, in his absence caused more billets to be laid into the cellar, as in his former examination he confessed, and returned about the end of August, or the beginning of September, and went again to the said house, near to the said cellar, and received the key of the cellar again of one of the five,[2] and then they brought in five or six barrels of powder more into the cellar, which also they covered with billets, saving four little barrels covered with fagots, and then this examinant went into the country about the end of September.

"It appeareth the powder was in the cellar placed as it was found the 5 of November, when the Lords came to prorogue the Parliament, and sayeth that he returned again to the said house near the cellar on Wednesday the 30 of October.

"*He confesseth he was at the Earl of Montgomery's marriage, but, as he sayeth, with no intention of evil having a sword about him, and was very near to his Majesty and the Lords there present.*[3]

[1] 'Thence,' in Stowe copy. [2] Percy.

[3] The words in italics are marked by penstrokes across them for omission.

"Forasmuch as they knew not well how they should come by the person of the Duke Charles, being near London, where they had no forces (if he had not been also blown up) he confesseth that it was resolved among them that, the same day that this detestable act should have been performed, the same day should other of their confederacy have surprised the person of the Lady Elizabeth, and presently have proclaimed her Queen, *to which purpose a proclamation was drawn, as well to avow and justify the action, as to have protested against the Union, and in no sort to have meddled with religion therein, and would have protested also against all strangers,* and this proclamation should have been made in the name of the Lady Elizabeth.

"Being demanded why they did not surprise the King's person, and draw him to the effecting of their purpose sayeth that so many must have been acquainted with such an action as it [1] would not have been kept secret.

"He confesseth that if their purpose had taken effect, until they had had power enough, they would not have avowed the deed to be theirs; but if their power (for their defence and safety) had been sufficient, they themselves would then [2] have taken it upon them. They meant also to have sent for the prisoners in the Tower to have come to them, of whom particularly they had some consultation.

"He confesseth that the place of rendezvous was in Warwickshire, and that armour was sent thither, but [3] the particular thereof [4] he knows not.

"He confesseth that they had consultation for the taking of the Lady Mary into their possession, but knew not how to come by her.

1 'With that practice, that,' in the Stowe copy.
2 'Then,' omitted in the Stowe copy.
3 'But,' omitted in the Stowe copy.
4 'Whereof,' in the Stowe copy.

"And confesseth that provision was made by some of the conspiracy of some armour of proof this last summer for this action.

"He confesseth that the powder was bought by the common purse of the confederates.

"L. Admiral [Earl of Nottingham] L. Chamberlain [Earl of Suffolk] Earl of Devonshire Earl of Northampton Earl of Salisbury Earl of Mar Lord Chief Justice [Popham] [1]	Attended by Mr. Attorney-General [Coke]."

Father Gerard, who has printed this examination in his Appendix,[2] styles it a draft, placing on the opposite pages the published confession of Guy Fawkes on November 17. That later confession, indeed, though embodying many passages of the earlier one, contains so many new statements, that it is a misapplication of words to speak of the one as the draft of the other. A probable explanation of the similarity is that when Fawkes was re-examined on the 17th, his former confession was produced, and he was required to supplement it with fresh information.

In one sense, indeed, the paper from which the examination of the 8th has been printed both by Father Gerard and myself, may be styled a draft, not of

[1] *G. P. B.*, No. 49. In the Stowe copy the names of the Commissioners are omitted, and a list of fifteen plotters added. As the paper was inclosed in a letter to Edmondes of the 14th, these might easily be added at any date preceding that.

[2] *Gerard*, p. 268.

the examination of the 17th, but of a copy forwarded to Edmondes on the 14th.[1] The two passages crossed out and printed above[2] in italics have been omitted in the copy intended for the ambassadors. All other differences, except those of punctuation, have been given in my notes, and it will be seen that they are merely the changes of a copyist from whom absolute verbal accuracy was not required. Father Gerard, indeed, says that in the original of the so-called draft five paragraphs were 'ticked off for omission.' He may be right, but in Winter's declaration of November 23, every paragraph is marked in the same way, and, at all events, not one of the five paragraphs is omitted in the copy sent to Edmondes.

In any other sense to call this paper a draft is to beg the whole question. What we want to know is whether it was a copy of the rough notes of the examination, signed by Fawkes himself, or a pure invention either of Salisbury or of the seven Commissioners and the Attorney-General. Curiously enough, one of the crossed out passages supplies evidence that the document is a genuine one. The first, indeed, proves nothing either way, and was, perhaps, left out merely because it was thought unwise to allow it to be known that the King had been so carelessly guarded that Percy had been admitted to his presence with a sword by his side. The second contains an intimation that the conspirators did not intend to rely only on a Catholic rising. They

[1] *Stowe MSS.*, 168, fol. 223. [2] *Gerard*, p. 170.

expected to have on their side Protestants who disliked the union with Scotland, and who were ready to protest 'against all strangers,' that is to say, against all Scots. We can readily understand that Privy Councillors, knowing as they did the line taken by the King in the matter of the union, would be unwilling to spread information of there being in England a Protestant party opposed to the union, not only of sufficient importance to be worth gaining, but so exasperated that even these gunpowder plotters could think it possible to win them to their side. Nor is this all. If it is difficult to conceive that the Commissioners could have allowed such a paragraph to go abroad, it is at least equally difficult to think of their inventing it. We may be sure that if Fawkes had not made the statement, no one of the examiners would ever have committed it to paper at all, and if the document is genuine in this respect, why is it not to be held genuine from beginning to end?

Father Gerard, indeed, objects to this view of the case that the document 'is unsigned; the list of witnesses is in the same handwriting as the rest, and in no instance is a witness indicated by such a title as he would employ for his signature. Throughout this paper Fawkes is made to speak in the third person, and the names of accomplices to whom he refers are not given.'[1] All this is quite true, and unless I am much mistaken, are evidences for the genuineness of

[1] *Gerard*, p. 169.

the document, not for its fabrication. If Salisbury had wished to palm off an invention of his own as a copy of a true confession by Fawkes, he surely would not have stuck at so small a thing as an alleged copy of the prisoner's signature, nor is it to be supposed that the original signatures of the Commissioners would appear in what, in my contention, is a copy of a lost original. As for the titles Lord Admiral and Lord Chamberlain being used instead of their signatures, it was in accordance with official usage. A letter, written on January 21, 1604–5, by the Council to the Judges, bears nineteen names at the foot in the place where signatures are ordinarily found. The first six names are given thus:—'L. Chancellor, L. Treasurer, L. Admirall, L. Chamberlaine, E. of Northumberland, E. of Worcester.'[1] Fawkes is made to speak in the third person in all the four preceding examinations, three of which bear his autograph signature. That the names of accomplices are not given is exactly what one might expect from a man of his courage. All through the five examinations he refused to break his oath not to reveal a name, except in the case of Percy in which concealment was impossible. It required the horrible torture of the 9th to wring a single name from him.

Moreover, Father Gerard further urges what he intends to be damaging to the view taken by me, that a set of questions formed by Coke upon the examination of the 7th, apparently for use on the 8th,

[1] *S. P. Dom.* xii. 24.

is 'not founded on information already obtained, but is, in fact, what is known as a "fishing document," intended to elicit evidence of some kind.'[1] Exactly so! If Coke had to fish, casting his net as widely as Father Gerard correctly shows him to have done, it is plain that the Government had no direct knowledge to guide its inquiries. Father Gerard's charge therefore resolves itself into this: that Salisbury not only deceived the public at large, but his brother-commissioners as well. Has he seriously thought out all that is involved in this theory? Salisbury, according to hypothesis, gets an altered copy of a confession drawn up, or else a confession purely invented by himself. The clerk who makes it is, of course, aware of what is being done, and also the second clerk[2] who wrote out the further copy sent to Edmondes. Edmondes, at least, received the second copy, and there can be little doubt that other ambassadors received it also. How could Salisbury count on the life-long silence of all these? Salisbury, as the event proved, was not exactly loved by his colleagues, and if his brother-commissioners—every one of them men of no slight influence at Court—had discovered that their names had been taken in vain, it would not have been left to the rumour of the streets to spread the news that Salisbury had been the inventor of the plot. Nay, more than this. Father Gerard distinctly sets down the story of the mine as an impossible one, and

[1] *Gerard*, p. 175. Coke's questions are in *S. P. Dom.* xvi. 38.

[2] The handwriting is quite different.

therefore one which must have been fabricated by Salisbury for his own purposes. The allegation that there had been a mine was not subsequently kept in the dark. It was proclaimed on the house-tops in every account of the plot published to the world. And all the while, it seems, six out of these seven Commissioners, to say nothing of the Attorney-General, knew that it was all a lie—that Fawkes, when they examined him on the 8th, had really said nothing about it, and yet, neither in public, nor, so far as we know, in private—either in Salisbury's lifetime or after his death—did they breathe a word of the wrong that had been done to them as well as to the conspirators!

CHAPTER III.

THE LATER DOCUMENTARY EVIDENCE.

HAVING thus, I hope, established that the story of the mine and cellar is borne out by Fawkes's own account, I proceed to examine into the objections raised by Father Gerard to the documentary evidence after November 8, the date of Fawkes's last examination before he was subjected to torture. In the declaration, signed with his tortured hand on the 9th, before Coke, Waad and Forsett,[1] and acknowledged before the Commissioners on the 10th, Fawkes distinctly refers to the examination of the 8th. "The plot," he says, "was to blow up the King with all the nobility about him in Parliament, as heretofore he hath declared, to which end, they proceeded as is set down in the examination taken (before the Lords of the Council Commissioners) yesternight." Here, then, is distinct evidence that Fawkes acknowledged that the examination of the 8th had been taken in presence of the Commissioners, and thus negatives the theory that that examination was invented or altered by Salisbury, as these words

[1] This declaration, therefore, was not, as Mrs. Everett Green says, 'made to Salisbury.'

came on the 10th under the eyes of the Commissioners themselves.[1]

The fact is, that the declaration of the 9th fits the examination of the 8th as a glove does a hand. On the 8th, before torture, Fawkes described what had been done, and gave the number of persons concerned in doing it. On the 9th he is required not to repeat what he had said before, but to give the missing names. This he now does. It was Thomas Winter who had fetched him from the Low Countries, having first communicated their design to a certain Owen.[2] The other three, who made up the original five, were Percy, Catesby, and John Wright. It was Gerard who had given them the Sacrament.[3] The other conspirators were Sir Everard Digby, Robert Keyes, Christopher Wright, Thomas[4] Grant, Francis Tresham, Robert Winter, and Ambrose Rokewood. The very order in which the names come

[1] If anyone chooses to argue that this examination was drawn up regardless of its truth, and only signed by Fawkes after torture had made him incapable of distinguishing truth from falsehood, he may be answered that, in that case, those who prepared it would never have added to the allegation that some of the conspirators had received the Sacrament from Gerard the Jesuit to bind them to secrecy, the passage:—"But he saith that Gerard was not acquainted with their purpose." This passage is marked for omission by Coke, and it assuredly would not have been found in the document unless it had really proceeded from Fawkes.

[2] About whom more hereafter.

[3] Gerard afterwards denied that this was true, and the late Father Morris (*Life of Gerard*, p. 437) argues, with a good deal of probability, that Fawkes mistook another priest for Gerard. For my purpose it is not a matter of any importance.

[4] This should be John.

perhaps shows that the Government had as yet a very hazy idea of the details of the conspiracy. The names of those who actually worked in the mine are scattered at hap-hazard amongst those of the men who merely countenanced the plot from a distance.

However this may be, the 9th, the day on which Fawkes was put to the torture, brought news to the Government that the fear of insurrection need no longer be entertained. It had been known before this that Fawkes's confederates had met on the 5th at Dunchurch on the pretext of a hunting match,[1] and had been breaking open houses in Warwickshire and Worcestershire in order to collect arms. Yet so indefinite was the knowledge of the Council that, on the 8th, they offered a reward for the apprehension of Percy alone, without including any of the other conspirators.[2] On the evening of the 9th[3] they received a letter from Sir Richard Walsh, the Sheriff of Worcestershire:—

"We think fit," he wrote, "with all speed to certify your Lordships of the happy success it hath pleased God to give us against the rebellious assembly in these parts. After such time as they had taken the horses from Warwick upon Tuesday night last,[4] they came to Mr. Robert Winter's house to Huddington upon Wednesday night,[5]

[1] Probably, as Father Gerard suggests, what would now be known as a coursing match.

[2] *Proclamation Book, R.O.* p. 117.

[3] A late postscript added to the letter to the Ambassadors sent off on the 9th (*Winwood*, ii. 173) shows that before the end of the day Salisbury had learnt even more of the details than were comprised in the Sheriff's letter.

[4] Nov. 5.

[5] Nov. 6.

where—having entered—[they] armed themselves at all points in open rebellion. They passed from thence upon Thursday morning[1] unto Hewell—the Lord Windsor's house—which they entered and took from thence by force great store of armour, artillery of the said Lord Windsor's, and passed that night into the county of Staffordshire unto the house of one Stephen Littleton, Gentleman, called Holbeche, about two miles distant from Stourbridge whither we pursued, with the assistance of Sir John Foliot, Knight, Francis Ketelsby, Esquire, Humphrey Salway, Gentleman, Edmund Walsh, and Francis Conyers, Gentlemen, with few other gentlemen and the power and face of the country. We made against them upon Thursday morning,[1] and freshly pursued them until the next day,[2] at which time about twelve or one of the clock in the afternoon, we overtook them at the said Holbeche House—the greatest part of their retinue and some of the better sort being dispersed and fled before our coming, whereupon and after summons and warning first given and proclamation in his Highness's name to yield and submit themselves—who refusing the same, we fired some part of the house and assaulted some part of the rebellious persons left in the said house, in which assault, one Mr. Robert Catesby is slain, and three others verily thought wounded to death whose names—as far as we can learn—are Thomas Percy, Gentleman, John Wright, and Christopher Wright Gentlemen, and these are apprehended and taken Thomas Winter Gentleman, John Grant Gentleman, Henry Morgan Gentleman, Ambrose Rokewood Gentleman, Thomas Ockley carpenter, Edmund Townsend servant to the said John Grant, Nicholas Pelborrow, servant unto the said Ambrose Rokewood, Edward Ockley carpenter, Richard Townsend servant to the said Robert Winter, Richard Day servant

[1] Nov. 7.   [2] Nov. 8.

to the said Stephen Littleton, which said prisoners are in safe custody here, and so shall remain until your Honours good pleasures be further known The rest of that rebellious assembly is dispersed, we have caused to be followed with fresh suite and hope of their speedy apprehension. We have also thought fit to send unto your Honours—according unto our duties—such letters as we have found about the parties apprehended ; and so resting in all duty at your Honours' further command, we take leave, from Stourbridge this Saturday morning, being the ixth of this instant November 1605.

Your Honours' most humble to be commanded,

RICH. WALSH.

Percy and the two Wrights died of their wounds, so that, in addition to Fawkes, Thomas Winter was the only one of the five original workers in the mine in the hands of the Government. Of the seven others who had been named in Fawkes's confession of the 9th, Christopher Wright had been killed ; Rokewood, Robert Winter, and Grant had been apprehended at Holbeche ; Sir Everard Digby, Keyes, and Tresham were subsequently arrested, as was Bates a servant of Catesby.

That for some days the Government made no effort to get further information about the mine and the cellar cannot be absolutely proved, but nothing bearing on the subject has reached us except that, on the 14th, when a copy of Fawkes's deposition of the 8th was forwarded to Edmondes, the names of the twelve chief conspirators are given, not as Fawkes gave them on the 9th, in two batches, but in three, Robert Winter and

Christopher Wright being said to have joined after the first five, whilst Rokewood, Digby, Grant, Tresham, and Keyes are said to have been 'privy to the practice of the powder but wrought not at the mine.'[1] As Keyes is the only one whose Christian name is not given, this list must have been copied from one now in the Record Office, in which this peculiarity is also found, and was probably drawn up on or about the 10th[2] from further information derived from Fawkes when he certified the confession dragged from him on the preceding day.[2]

What really seems to have been at this time on the minds of the investigators was the relationship of the Catholic noblemen to the plot. On the 11th Talbot of Grafton was sent for. On the 15th Lords Montague and Mordaunt were imprisoned in the Tower. On the 16th Mrs. Vaux and the wives of ten of the conspirators were committed to various aldermen and merchants of London.[3] When Fawkes was re-examined on the 16th,[4] by far the larger part of the answers elicited refer to the hints given, or supposed to have been given, to Catholic noblemen to absent themselves from Parliament

[1] The question whether Winter or Keyes was one of two workers will be subsequently discussed.

[2] Mrs. Everett Green suggests Nov. 8 (*G. P. B.* No. 133), but this is merely a deduction from her mistaken date of the examination of the 17th (see p. 17, note 1). In Fawkes's confession of the 9th Keyes's Christian name appears to have been subsequently added.

[3] Extracts from the Council Registers, *Add. MSS.* 11,402, fol. 108. The volume of the Council Book itself which recorded the transactions of these years has been lost.

[4] *G. P. B.* No. 101. There is a facsimile in *National MSS.* Part iv. No. 8.

on the 5th. Then comes a statement about Percy buying a watch for Fawkes on the night of the 4th and sending it 'to him by Keyes at ten of the clock at night, because he should know how the time went away.' The last paragraph alone bears upon the project itself. "He also saith he did not intend to set fire to the train [until] the King was come to the House, and then he purposed to do it with a piece of touchwood and with a match also, *which were about him when he was apprehended on the 4th day of November at* 11 *of the clock at night* that the powder might more surely take fire a quarter of an hour after."

The words printed in italics are an interlineation in Coke's hand. They evidently add nothing of the slightest importance to the evidence, and cannot have been inserted with any design to prejudice the prisoner or to carry conviction in quarters in which disbelief might be supposed to exist. Is not the simple explanation sufficient, that when the evidence was read over to the examinee, he added, either of his own motion or on further question, this additional information. If this explanation is accepted here, may it not also be accepted for other interlineations, such as that relating to the cellar in the first examination?[1]

That the examiners at this stage of the proceedings should not be eager to ask further questions about the cellar and the mine was the most natural thing in the world. They knew already

[1] See pp. 18, 20.

quite enough from Fawkes's earlier examinations to put them in possession of the general features of the plot, and to them it was of far greater interest to trace out its ramifications, and to discover whether a guilty knowledge of it could be brought home either to noblemen or to priests, than to attain to a descriptive knowledge of its details, which would be dear to the heart of the newspaper correspondent of the present day. Yet, after all, even in 1605, the public had to be taken into account. There must be an open trial, and the more detailed the information that could be got the more verisimilitude would be given to the story told. It is probably, in part at least, to these considerations, as well as to some natural curiosity on the part of the Commissioners themselves, that we owe the examinations of Fawkes on the 17th and of Winter on the 23rd.

"Amongst all the confessions and 'voluntary declarations' extracted from the conspirators," writes Father Gerard, "there are two of exceptional importance, as having furnished the basis of the story told by the Government, and ever since generally accepted. These are a long declaration made by Thomas Winter, and another by Guy Fawkes, which alone were made public, being printed in the 'King's Book,' and from which are gathered the essential particulars of the story, as we are accustomed to hear it."

If Father Gerard merely means that the story published by the Government rested on these two confessions, and that the Government publications were the source of all knowledge about the plot till the Record Office was thrown open, in comparatively recent years, he says what is perfectly true, and, it may be added, quite irrelevant. If he means that our knowledge at the present day rests on these two documents, he is, as I hope I have already shown, mistaken. With the first five examinations of Fawkes in our hands, all the essential points of the conspiracy, except the names, are revealed to us. The names are given in the examination under torture, and a day or two later the Government was able to classify these names, though we are unable to specify the source from which it drew its information. If both the declarations to which Father Gerard refers had been absolutely destroyed we should have missed some picturesque details, which assist us somewhat in understanding what took place; but we should have been able to set forth the main features of the plot precisely as we do now.

Nevertheless, as we do gain some additional information from these documents, let us examine whether there are such symptoms of foul play as Father Gerard thinks he can descry. Taking first Fawkes's declaration of November 17, it will be well to follow Father Gerard's argument. He brings into collocation three documents: first the interrogatories prepared by Coke after the examination of the 7th, then the examination of the 8th, which he calls a draft, and then the full declaration of the 17th, which undoubtedly bears the signature of Fawkes himself.

That the three documents are very closely connected is undeniable. Take, for instance, a paragraph to which

Father Gerard not unnaturally draws attention, in which the repetition of the words 'the same day' proves at least partial identity of origin between Coke's interrogatories and the examination founded on them on the 8th.[1]

"Was it not agreed," asks Coke, "the same day that the act should have been done, the same day, or soon after, the person of the Lady Elizabeth should have been surprised?" "He confesseth," Fawkes is stated to have said, "that the same day this detestable act should have been performed the same day should other of their confederacy have surprised the Lady Elizabeth." Yet before setting down Fawkes's replies as a fabrication of the Government, let us remember how evidence of this kind is taken and reported. If we take up the report of a criminal trial in a modern newspaper we shall find, for the most part, a flowing narrative put into the mouths of witnesses. John Jones, let us say, is represented as giving some such evidence as this: "I woke at two o'clock in the morning, and, looking out of window, saw by the light of the moon John Smith opening the stable door," &c. Nobody who has attended a law court imagines John Jones to have used these consecutive words. Questions are put to him by the examining counsel. When did you wake? Did you see anyone at the stable door? How came you to be able to see him, and so forth; and it is by combining these questions with the Yes and No, and other brief replies made by the

[1] *Gerard*, p. 174.

witness, that the reporter constructs his narrative with no appreciable violation of truth. Is it not reasonable to suppose that the same practice prevailed in 1605? Fawkes, I suppose, answered to Coke's question, "Yes, others of the confederates proposed to surprise her," or something of the sort, and the result was the combination of question and answer which is given above.

What, however, was the relation between the examination of the 8th and the declaration of the 17th? Father Gerard has printed them side by side,[1] and it is impossible to deny that the latter is founded on the former. Some paragraphs of the examination are not represented in the declaration, but these are paragraphs of no practical importance, and those that are represented are modified. The modifications admitted, however, are all consistent with what is a very probable supposition, that the Government wanted to get Fawkes's previous statements collected in one paper. He had given his account of the plot on one occasion, the names of the plotters on another, and had stated on a third that they were to be classified in three divisions—those who worked first at the mine, those who worked at it afterwards, and those who did not work at all. If the Government drew up a form combining the three statements and omitting immaterial matter, and got Fawkes to sign it, this would fully account for the form in which we find the declaration At the present day, we should object to receive evi-

[1] *Gerard*, p. 268.

dence from a man who had been tortured once and might be tortured again; but as this declaration adds nothing of any importance to our previous knowledge, it is unnecessary to recur to first principles on this occasion.[1]

Winter's examination of the 23rd, as treated by Father Gerard, raises a more difficult question. The document itself is at Hatfield, and there is a copy of it in the 'Gunpowder Plot Book' in the Public Record Office. "The 'original' document," writes Father Gerard,[2] "is at Hatfield, and agrees in general so exactly with the copy as to demonstrate the identity of their origin. But while, as we have seen, the 'copy' is dated November 23rd, the 'original' is dated on the 25th." In a note, we are told 'that this is not a slip of the pen is evidenced by the fact that Winter first wrote 23, and then corrected it to 25.' To return to Father Gerard's text, we find, "On a circumstance so irregular, light is possibly thrown by a letter from Waad, the Lieutenant of the Tower, to Cecil[3] on the 20th of the same month. 'Thomas Winter,' he wrote, 'doth find his hand so strong, as after dinner he will settle himself to write that he hath verbally declared to your Lordship, adding what he shall remember.' The inference is certainly suggested that torture had been used until the prisoner's

[1] The erasure of Winter's name, and the substitution of that of Keyes, will be dealt with later.

[2] *Gerard*, p. 168.

[3] Father Gerard appears to show his dislike of Salisbury by denying him his title.

spirit was sufficiently broken to be ready to tell the story required of him, and that the details were furnished by those who demanded it. It must, moreover. be remarked that, although Winter's 'original' declaration is witnessed only by Sir E. Coke, the Attorney-General, it appears in print attested by all those whom Cecil had selected for the purpose two days before the declaration was made."

Apparently Father Gerard intends us to gather from his statement that the whole confession of Winter was drawn up by the Government on or before the 23rd, and that he was driven on the 25th by fears of renewed torture to put his hand to a tissue of falsehoods contained in a paper which the Government required him to copy out and sign. The whole of this edifice, it will be seen, rests on the assertion that Winter first wrote 23 and then corrected it to 25.

So improbable did this assertion appear to me, that I wrote to Mr. Gunton, the courteous secretary of the Marquis of Salisbury, requesting him to examine the handwriting of the date in question. He tells me that the confession itself is, as Father Gerard states, in Winter's hand, as is also the date '23 9ber 1605.' Two changes have been made; in the first place 23 has been altered to 25, and there has been added at the head of the paper: "The voluntary declaration of Thomas Winter, of Hoodington, in the County of Worcester, gent. the 25 of November, 1605." "This heading," Mr. Gunton writes, "is so tucked in at the top, that it must, I think, have been written after the confession itself." He also assures me that the 5 of the substituted date and the 5 in the added heading 'are exactly alike, and both different from the 5' at the end of the date of the year, as written by Winter. "The heading," Mr. Gunton writes, "I believe to be in Coke's hand. It is more carefully written than he usually writes, and more carefully than his attestation at the end; but as far as my judgment goes, it is decidedly his hand."

The alleged fact that lies at the basis of Father Gerard's argument is therefore finally disposed of. Why Coke, if Coke it was, changed the date can be no more than matter for conjecture. Yet an explanation, conjectural though it be, seems to me to be probable enough. We have seen that Fawkes's confession under torture bears two dates, the 9th, when it was taken before Coke and Waad the Lieutenant of the Tower, together with a magistrate, Edward Forsett; the second, on the 10th, when it was declared before the Commissioners. Why may not this confession of Winter's have been subjected to a similar process. Winter, I suppose, writes it on the 23rd, and it is then witnessed, as Father Gerard says, by Coke alone. Though no copy with the autograph signatures of the Commissioners exists it is reasonable to suppose that one was made, in which a passage about Monteagle—whom the Government did not wish to connect with the plot except as a discoverer—was omitted, and that this, still bearing the date of the 23rd, may have been brought before the Commissioners on the 25th. They would thus receive a statement from Winter that it was his own, and the signatures of the Commissioners would then be appended to it, together with those of Coke and Waad. This then would be the document from which copies would be taken for the use of individual Commissioners, and we can thus account for Salisbury's having appended to his own copy now in the Record Office, "Taken before us, Nottingham, Suffolk, &c." The recognition before the Commissioners would become the official date, and Coke, having access to the original, changes the date on which it was written to that on which it was signed by the Commissioners. This explanation is merely put forward as a possible one. The important point is that Father Gerard's argument founded on the alteration of the date is inadmissible, now that Mr. Gunton has thrown light on the matter.

Winter's confession having been thus vindicated is here inserted, partly because it gives the story from a different point of view from that of Fawkes, and partly because it will enable those who read it to see for themselves whether there is internal evidence of its having been manipulated by the Government.

My Most Honourable Lords.

"23 9 ber 1605.

"Not out of hope to obtain pardon for speaking—of my temporal part I may say the fault is greater than can be forgiven—nor affecting hereby the title of a good subject for I must redeem my country from as great a danger as I have hazarded the bringing her into, before I can purchase any such opinion ; only at your Honours' command, I will briefly set down my own accusation, and how far I have proceeded in this business which I shall the faithfuller do, since I see such courses are not pleasing to Almighty God ; and that all, or the most material parts have been already confessed.

"I remained with my brother in the country for Allhollantide,[1] in the year of our Lord 1603, the first of the King's reign, about which time, Mr. Catesby sent thither, entreating me to come to London, where he and other friends would be glad to see me. I desired him to excuse me, for I found not myself very well disposed, and (which had happened never to me before) returned the messenger without my company. Shortly I received another letter, in any wise to come. At the second summons I presently came up and found him with Mr. John Wright at Lambeth, where he brake with me how necessary it was not to forsake my country (for he knew I had then a resolution to go over), but to deliver her from the servitude in which she remained, or at least to assist her with our uttermost endeavours. I answered that I had often hazarded my life upon far lighter terms, and now would not refuse any good occasion wherein I might do service to the Catholic cause ; but, for myself, I knew no mean probable to succeed. He said that he had bethought him of a way at one instant to deliver us from all our bonds, and without any foreign help [2] to replant again the Catholic religion, and

[1] All Saints Day.

[2] Compare this with Fawkes's declaration at his second examination (*G. P. B.* 16, A.) "Being demanded when this good act had been done which must have brought this realm in peril to be subdued by

withal told me in a word it was to blow up the Parliament House with gunpowder ; for, said he, in that place have they done us all the mischief, and perchance God hath designed that place for their punishment. I wondered at the strangeness of the conceit, and told him that true it was this strake at the root and would breed a confusion fit to beget new alterations, but if it should not take effect (as most of this nature miscarried) the scandal would be so great which the Catholic religion might hereby sustain, as not only our enemies, but our friends also would with good reason condemn us. He told me the nature of the disease required so sharp a remedy, and asked me if I would give my consent. I told him Yes, in this or what else soever, if he resolved upon it, I would venture my life ; but I proposed many difficulties, as want of a house, and of one to carry the mine ; noise in the working, and such like. His answer was, let us give an attempt, and where it faileth, pass no further. But first, quoth he, because we will leave no peaceable and quiet way untried, you shall go over and inform the Constable [1] of the state of the Catholics here in England, intreating him to solicit his Majesty at his coming hither that the penal laws may be recalled, and we

some foreign prince, of what foreign prince he and his compliees could have wished to have been governed, one more than another, he doth protest upon his soul that neither he nor any other with whom he had conferred would have spared the last drop of their blood to have resisted any foreign prince whatsoever." Are we seriously asked to believe that Salisbury placed this crown of sturdy patriotism on the brows of those whom he wished to paint as the most atrocious villains ?

[1] Juan de Velasco, Duke of Frias, Constable of Castile, arrived at Brussels about the middle of January 1604 to conduct a negotiation for peace with England. There he remained, delegating his powers to others. This date of the Constable's arrival is important, as showing that Winter's conversation with Catesby cannot have taken place earlier than the second half of January.

admitted into the rank of his other subjects. Withal, you may bring over some confidant gentleman such as you shall understand best able for this business, and named unto me Mr. Fawkes. Shortly after I passed the sea and found the Constable at Bergen, near Dunkirk, where, by the help of Mr. Owen,[1] I delivered my message, whose answer was that he had strict command from his master to do all good offices for the Catholics, and for his own part he thought himself bound in conscience so to do, and that no good occasion should be omitted, but spake to him nothing of this matter.

"Returning to Dunkirk with Mr. Owen, we had speach whether he thought the Constable would faithfully help us or no. He said he believed nothing less, and that they sought only their own ends, holding small account of Catholics. I told him, that there were many gentlemen in England, who would not forsake their country until they had tried the uttermost, and rather venture their lives than forsake her in this misery; and to add one more to our number as a fit man, both for counsel and execution of whatsoever we should resolve, wished for Mr. Fawkes whom I had heard good commendations of. He told me the gentleman deserved no less, but was at Brussels, and that if he came not, as happily he might, before my departure, he would send him shortly after into England. I went soon after to Ostend, where Sir William Stanley as then was not, but came two days after. I remained with

[1] Hugh Owen was, as Father Gerard says (p. 173, note 1), 'A soldier and not a priest, though in the *Calendar of State Papers* he is continually styled "Father Owen," or "Owen the Jesuit."' He is however mistaken in saying that Mrs. Everett Green inserted the title without warrant in the original documents. A paper of intelligence received on April 29, 1604, begins, "Father Owen, Father Baldwin and Colonel Jaques, three men that rule the Archduke at their pleasure," &c.

him three or four days, in which time I asked him, if the Catholics in England should do anything to help themselves, whether he thought the Archduke would second them. He answered, No; for all those parts were so desirous of peace with England as they would endure no speach of other enterprise, neither were it fit, said he, to set any project afoot now the peace is upon concluding. I told him there was no such resolution, and so fell to discourse of other matters until I came to speak of Mr. Fawkes whose company I wished over into England. I asked of his sufficiency in the wars, and told him we should need such as he, if occasion required. He gave very good commendations of him; and as we were thus discoursing and I ready to depart for Nieuport and taking my leave of Sir William, Mr. Fawkes came into our company newly returned and saluted us. This is the gentleman, said Sir William, that you wished for, and so we embraced again. I told him some good friends of his wished his company in England; and that if he pleased to come to Dunkirk, we would have further conference, whither I was then going: so taking my leave of both, I departed. About two days after came Mr. Fawkes to Dunkirk, where I told him that we were upon a resolution to do somewhat in England if the peace with Spain helped us not, but had as yet resolved upon nothing. Such or the like talk we passed at Gravelines, where I lay for a wind, and when it served, came both in one passage to Greenwich, near which place we took a pair of oars, and so came up to London, and came to Mr. Catesby whom we found in his lodging. He welcomed us into England, and asked me what news from the Constable. I told him Good words, but I feared the deeds would not answer. This was the beginning of Easter term [1] and about the midst of the same term (whether sent for

[1] In 1604 Easter term began on April 25, and ended May 21.

by Mr. Catesby, or upon some business of his own) up came Mr. Thomas Percy. The first word he spake (after he came into our company) was Shall we always, gentlemen, talk and never do anything? Mr. Catesby took him aside and had speech about somewhat to be done, so as first we might all take an oath of secrecy, which we resolved within two or three days to do, so as there we met behind St. Clement's, Mr. Catesby, Mr. Percy, Mr. Wright, Mr. Guy Fawkes, and myself, and having, upon a primer given each other the oath of secrecy in a chamber where no other body was, we went after into the next room and heard mass, and received the blessed sacrament upon the same. Then did Mr. Catesby disclose to Mr. Percy,[1] and I together with Jack Wright tell to Mr. Fawkes the business for which they took this oath which they both approved; and then Mr. Percy sent to take the house, which Mr. Catesby, in my absence, had learnt did belong to one Ferris, which with some difficulty in the end he obtained, and became, as Ferris before was, tenant to Whynniard. Mr. Fawkes underwent the name of Mr. Percy's man, calling himself Johnson, because his face was the most unknown,[2] and received the keys of the house, until we heard

[1] This distinctly implies that Percy did not know the secret before, and I therefore wish to retract my former argument—which is certainly not conclusive—in favour of an earlier knowledge by Percy. *Hist. of Engl.* 1603–1642, i. 235, note 1.

[2] "In his declaration, November 8th, however," writes Father Gerard (p. 91, note 1), "he gives as a reason for going abroad, 'lest, being a dangerous man, he should be known and suspected.'" I see no discrepancy between the two statements. Having been long abroad, Fawkes's face would not be known to the ordinary Londoner as that of a Recusant, and he was therefore better qualified to act as a watchman than others who were so known. On the other hand, when there was no need for anybody to watch at all, somebody who had known him in Flanders might notify the Government of his

that the Parliament was adjourned to the 7 of February. At which time we all departed several ways into the country, to meet again at the beginning of Michaelmas term.[1] Before this time also it was thought convenient to have a house that might answer to Mr. Percy's, where we might make provision of powder and wood for the mine which, being there made ready, should in a night be conveyed by boat to the house by the Parliament because we were loth to foil that with often going in and out. There was none that we could devise so fit as Lambeth where Mr. Catesby often lay, and to be keeper thereof, by Mr. Catesby's choice, we received into the number Keyes, as a trusty honest man.[2]

"Some fortnight after, towards the beginning of the term, Mr. Fawkes and I came to Mr. Catesby at Moorcrofts, where we agreed that now was time to begin and set things in order for the mine, so as Mr. Fawkes went to London and the next day sent for me to come over to him. When I came, the cause was for that the Scottish Lords were appointed to sit in conference on the Union in Mr. Percy's house. This hindered our beginning until a fortnight before Christmas, by which time both Mr. Percy and Mr. Wright were come to London, and we against their coming had provided a good part of the powder, so as we all five entered with tools fit to begin our work, having provided ourselves of baked-meats, the less to need sending abroad. We entered late in the night, and were never seen, save only Mr. Percy's man, until Christmas-eve, in which time we wrought under a little entry to the

appearance in England, and thereby raise suspicions against him. Besides, there were other reasons for his going over which Fawkes did not think fit to bring to the notice of the Government.

[1] Began October 9, ended November 28.

[2] Marginal note: "This was about a month before Michaelmas."

wall of the Parliament House, and underpropped it as we went with wood.

"Whilst we were together we began to fashion our business, and discourse what we should do after this deed were done. The first question was how we might surprise the next heir; the Prince happily would be at the Parliament with the King his father: how should we then be able to seize on the Duke?[1] This burden Mr. Percy undertook; that by his acquaintance he with another gentleman would enter the chamber without suspicion, and having some dozen others at several doors to expect his coming, and two or three on horseback at the Court gate to receive him, he would undertake (the blow being given, until which he would attend in the Duke's chamber) to carry him safe away, for he supposed most of the Court would be absent, and such as were there not suspecting, or unprovided for any such matter. For the Lady Elizabeth it were easy to surprise her in the country by drawing friends together at a hunting near the Lord Harrington's, and Ashby, Mr. Catesby's house, being not far off was a fit place for preparation.

"The next was for money and horses, which if we could provide in any reasonable measure (having the heir apparent) and the first knowledge by four or five days was odds sufficient. Then, what Lords we should save from the Parliament, which was agreed in general as many as we could that were Catholics or so disposed. Next, what foreign princes we should acquaint with this before or join with after. For this point we agreed that first we would not enjoin princes to that secrecy nor oblige them by oath so to be secure of their promise; besides, we know not whether they will approve the project or dislike it, and if they do allow thereof, to prepare before might beget

[1] The Duke of York, afterwards Charles I.

suspicion and [1] not to provide until the business were acted; the same letter that carried news of the thing done might as well entreat their help and furtherance. Spain is too slow in his preparations to hope any good from in the first extremities, and France too near and too dangerous, who with the shipping of Holland we feared of all the world might make away with us. But while we were in the middle of these discourses, we heard that the Parliament should be anew adjourned until after Michaelmas, upon which tidings we broke off both discourse and working until after Christmas. About Candlemas we brought over in a boat the powder which we had provided at Lambeth and layd it in Mr. Percy's house because we were willing to have all our danger in one place. We wrought also another fortnight in the mine against the stone wall, which was very hard to beat through, at which time we called in Kit Wright, and near to Easter [2] as we wrought the third time, opportunity was given to hire the cellar, in which we resolved to lay the powder and leave the mine.

"Now by reason that the charge of maintaining us all so long together, besides the number of several houses which for several uses had been hired, and buying of powder, &c., had lain heavy on Mr. Catesby alone to support, it was necessary for to call in some others to ease his charge, and to that end desired leave that he with Mr. Percy and a third whom they should call might acquaint whom they thought fit and willing to the business, for many, said he, may be content that I should know who would not therefore that all the Company should be acquainted with their names. To this we all agreed.

"After this Mr. Fawkes laid into the cellar (which he had newly taken) a thousand of billets and five hundred of

[1] Some such words as 'we resolved' are probably omitted here.

[2] In MS. 'taken it before.'

faggots, and with that covered the powder, because we might have the house free to suffer anyone to enter that would. Mr. Catesby wished us to consider whether it were not now necessary to send Mr. Fawkes over, both to absent himself for a time as also to acquaint Sir William Stanley and Mr. Owen with this matter. We agreed that he should ; provided that he gave it them with the same oath that we had taken before, viz., to keep it secret from all the world. The reason why we desired Sir William Stanley should be acquainted herewith was to have him with us so soon as he could, and, for Mr. Owen, he might hold good correspondency after with foreign princes. So Mr. Fawkes departed about Easter for Flanders and returned the later end of August. He told me that when he arrived at Brussels, Sir William Stanley was not returned from Spain, so as he uttered the matter only to Owen, who seemed well pleased with the business, but told him that surely Sir William would not be acquainted with any plot as having business now afoot in the Court of England, but he himself would be always ready to tell it him and send him away so soon as it were done.

"About this time did Mr. Percy and Mr. Catesby meet at the Bath where they agreed that the company being yet but few, Mr. Catesby should have the others' authority to call in whom he thought best, by which authority he called in after Sir Everard Digby, though at what time I know not, and last of all Mr. Francis Tresham. The first promised, as I heard Mr. Catesby say, fifteen hundred pounds. Mr. Percy himself promised all that he could get of the Earl of Northumberland's rent,[1] and to provide many galloping horses, his number was ten.[2] Meanwhile Mr. Fawkes and

[1] Interlined in the King's hand 'which was about four thousand pounds.'

[2] Altered in the King's hand to 'to the number of ten,' with a marginal note 'unclear phrase,' in the same hand.

myself alone bought some new powder, as suspecting the first to be dank, and conveyed it into the cellar and set it in order as we resolved it should stand. Then was the Parliament anew prorogued until the 5 of November; so as we all went down until some ten days before. When Mr. Catesby came up with Mr. Fawkes to a house by Enfield Chase called White Webbs, whither I came to them, and Mr. Catesby willed me to inquire whether the young Prince[1] came to Parliament, I told him that his Grace thought not to be there. Then must we have our horses, said Mr. Catesby, beyond the water,[2] and provision of more company to surprise the Prince and leave the Duke alone. Two days after, being Sunday[3] at night, in came one to my chamber and told me that a letter had been given to my Lord Monteagle to this effect, that he wished his lordship's absence from the Parliament because a blow would there be given, which letter he presently carried to my Lord of Salisbury. On the morrow I went to White Webbs and told it to Mr. Catesby, assuring him withal that the matter was disclosed and wishing him in any wise to forsake his country. He told me he would see further as yet and resolved to send Mr. Fawkes to try the uttermost, protesting if the part belonged to myself he would try the same adventure. On Wednesday Mr. Fawkes went and returned at night, of which we were very glad. Thursday[4] I came to London, and Friday[5] Mr. Catesby, Mr. Tresham and I met at Barnet, where we questioned how this letter should be sent to my Lord Monteagle, but could not conceive, for Mr. Tresham forsware it, whom we only suspected. On Saturday night[6] I met Mr. Tresham again in Lincoln's Inn Walks, where he told such speeches that my Lord of Salisbury should use to

[1] Prince Henry.

[2] Perhaps the Prince was with his mother at Greenwich.

[3] Oct. 27. [4] Oct. 31. [5] Nov. 1. [6] Nov. 2.

the King, as I gave it lost the second time, and repeated the same to Mr. Catesby, who hereupon was resolved to be gone, but stayed to have Mr. Percy come up whose consent herein we wanted. On Sunday night [1] came Mr. Percy, and no 'Nay,' but would abide the uttermost trial.

"This suspicion of all hands put us into such confusion as Mr. Catesby resolved to go down into the country the Monday [2] that Mr. Percy went to Sion and Mr. Percy resolved to follow the same night or early the next morning. About five o'clock being Tuesday [3] came the younger Wright to my chamber and told me that a nobleman called the Lord Monteagle, saying "Rise and come along to Essex House, for I am going to call up my Lord of Northumberland," saying withal 'the matter is discovered.' "Go back Mr. Wright," quoth I, "and learn what you can at Essex Gate." Shortly he returned and said, "Surely all is lost, for Leyton is got on horseback at Essex door, and as he parted, he asked if their Lordship's would have any more with him, and being answered "No," is rode as fast up Fleet Street as he can ride." "Go you then," quoth I, "to Mr. Percy, for sure it is for him they seek, and bid him begone: I will stay and see the uttermost." Then I went to the Court gates, and found them straitly guarded so as nobody could enter. From thence I went down towards the Parliament House, and in the middle of King's Street found the guard standing that would not let me pass, and as I returned, I heard one say, "There is a treason discovered in which the King and the Lords shall have been blown up," so then I was fully satisfied that all was known, and went to the stable where my gelding stood, and rode into the country. Mr. Catesby had appointed our meeting at Dunchurch, but I could not overtake them until I came to my brother's which was Wednesday night.[4] On Thurs-

[1] Nov. 3. [2] Nov. 4. [3] 5 A.M. on Nov. 5. [4] Nov. 6.

day[1] we took the armour at my Lord Windsor's, and went that night to one Stephen Littleton's house, where the next day, being Friday,[2] as I was early abroad to discover, my man came to me and said that a heavy mischance had severed all the company, for that Mr. Catesby, Mr. Rokewood and Mr. Grant were burnt with gunpowder, upon which sight the rest dispersed. Mr. Littleton wished me to fly and so would he. I told him I would first see the body of my friend and bury him, whatsoever befel me. When I came I found Mr. Catesby reasonable well, Mr. Percy, both the Wrights, Mr. Rokewood and Mr. Grant. I asked them what they resolved to do. They answered "We mean here to die." I said again I would take such part as they did. About eleven of the clock came the company to beset the house, and as I walked into the court was shot into the shoulder, which lost me the use of my arm. The next shot was the elder Wright struck dead; after him the younger Mr. Wright, and fourthly Ambrose Rokewood. Then, said Mr. Catesby to me (standing before the door they were to enter), "Stand by, Mr. Tom, and we will die together." "Sir," quoth I, "I have lost the use of my right arm and I fear that will cause me to be taken." So as we stood close together Mr. Catesby, Mr. Percy and myself, they two were shot (as far as I could guess, with one bullet), and then the company entered upon me, hurt me in the belly with a pike and gave me other wounds, until one came behind and caught hold of both my arms, and so I remain, Your &c."

"[Taken before us

"Nottingham, Suffolk, Northampton, Salisbury, Mar, Dunbar, Popham.

EDW. COKE,
W. WAAD.]"[3]

[1] Nov. 7.
[2] Nov. 8.
[3] The attestation in brackets is in Salisbury's hand.

I have printed this interesting statement in full, because it is the only way in which I can convey to my readers the sense of spontaneity which pervades it from beginning to end. To me, at least, it seems incredible that it was either written to order, or copied from a paper drawn up by some agent of the Government. Nor is it to be forgotten that if there was one thing the Government was anxious to secure, it was evidence against the priests, and that no such evidence can be extracted from this confession. What is, perhaps, still more to the point is, that no candid person can, I imagine, rise from the perusal of these sentences without having his estimate of the character of the conspirators raised. There is no conscious assumption of high qualities, but each touch as it comes strengthens the belief that the men concerned in the plot were patient and loyal, brave beyond the limits of ordinary bravery, and utterly without selfish aims. Could this result have been attained by a confession written to order or dictated by Salisbury or his agents, to whom the plotters were murderous villains of the basest kind ?

There is nothing to show that Winter's evidence was procured by torture. Father Gerard, indeed, quotes a letter from Waad, written on the 21st, in which he says that 'Thomas Winter doth find his hand so strong as after dinner he will settle himself to write that he hath verbally declared to your Lordship adding what he shall remember.' Considering that he had a ball through his shoulder a fortnight before, the suggestion of torture is hardly needed to find a cause for his having for some time been unable to use his hand.

Before turning to another branch of the investigation, it will be advisable to clear up one difficulty which is not quite so easy to solve.

"Fawkes," writes Father Gerard,[1] "in the confession of November 17, mentioned Robert Keyes as amongst the first seven of the conspirators who worked at the mine, and Robert Winter as one of the five introduced at a later period. The names of these two were deliberately interchanged in the published version, Robert Winter appearing as a worker in the mine, and Keyes, who was an obscure man, of no substance, among the gentlemen of property whose resources were to have supported the subsequent rebellion. Moreover, in the account of the same confession sent to Edmondes by Cecil three days before Fawkes signed it—*i.e.*, November 14—the same transposition occurs, Keyes being explicitly described as one of those 'who wrought not at the mine,' although, as we have seen, he is one of the three who alone make any mention of it.

"Still more irregular is another circumstance. About November 28, Sir Edward Coke, the Attorney-General, drew up certain further notes of questions to be put to various prisoners. Amongst these we read: 'Winter[2] to be examined of his brother, for no man else can accuse him.' But a fortnight or so before this time the Secretary of State had officially informed the ambassador in the Low Countries that Robert Winter was one of those deepest in the treason, and, to say nothing of other evidence, a proclamation for his apprehension had been issued on November 18th. Yet Coke's interrogatory seems to imply that nothing had yet been established against him, and

[1] *Gerard*, p. 182. [2] *I.e.*, Thomas Winter.

that he was not known to the general body of the traitors as a fellow-conspirator."

If this tangled skein is to be unravelled, the first thing to be done is to place the facts in their chronological order, upon which many if not all the difficulties will disappear, premising that, as a matter of fact, Keyes did work at the mine, and Robert Winter did not.

In his examination of November 7, in which no names appear, and nothing is said about a mine, Fawkes spoke of five original conspirators, and of five or six subsequently joining them, and being generally acquainted with the plot.[1] On the 8th,[2] when the mine was first mentioned, he divided the seven actual diggers into two classes: first, the five who worked from the beginning, and, secondly, two who were afterwards added to that number, saying nothing of the conspirators who took no part in the mining operations. On the 9th, under torture, he gave the names of the first five apart, and then lumped all the other conspirators together, so that both Keyes and Robert Winter appear in the same class. On the 17th he gave, as the names of two, who, as he now said, subsequently worked at the mine, Christopher Wright and Robert Winter, but the surname of the latter

[1] Mrs. Everett Green's abstract of this, to the effect that Fawkes said that the conspiracy 'was confined to five persons at first, then to two, and afterwards five more were added,' has no foundation in the document she had before her.

[2] *G. P. B.* No. 49.

is deleted with pen-strokes, and that of Keyes substituted above it; whilst, in the list of the persons made privy to the plot but not engaged in digging, we have the name of Keyes, afterwards deleted, and that of Wynter substituted for it.[1] The only question is, when was the double substitution effected?

As far as the action of the Government is known, we have the list referred to at pp. 47, 48, and probably written on or about the 10th.[2] In this the additional workers are first said to have been John Grant and Christopher Wright. The former name is, however, scratched out, and that of 'Robyn Winter' substituted for it, and from this list is taken the one forwarded to Edmondes on the 14th.[3] Even if we could discover any conceivable motive for the Government wishing to accuse Keyes rather than Winter, it would not help us to explain why the name of Winter was substituted for that of Grant at one time, and the name of Keyes substituted for that of Winter at another.

On the other hand, Fawkes, if he had any knowledge of what was going on, had at least a probable motive for putting Winter rather than Keyes in the worse category. Keyes had been seized, whilst Winter was still at large, and Fawkes may have thought that as Winter might make his escape beyond sea, it was better to load him with the burden which really belonged

[1] *G. P. B.* No. 37. [2] *G. P. B.* No. 133.

[3] The name 'Key' or 'Keyes' occurs in both of them without his Christian name.

to Keyes. If this solution be accepted as a possible one, it is easy to understand how the Government fixed on Winter as one of the actual diggers. On the 18th, the day after his name had been given by Fawkes, a proclamation is issued for his apprehension as one 'known to be a principal.'[1] It is not for ten days that any sign is given of a belief that Keyes was the right man. Then, on the 28th, Coke suggests that Thomas Winter may be examined about his brother, 'for no man else can accuse him,' a suggestion which would be absurd if Fawkes's statement had still held good. On the 30th Keyes himself acknowledges that he bought some of the powder and assisted in carrying it to Ferrers' house, and that he also helped to work at the mine.

I am inclined therefore to assign the alteration of the name which Fawkes gave in his examination of the 17th to some day shortly before the 28th, and to think that the sending of the 'King's Book'[2] to press took place on some day between the 23rd, the date of Thomas Winter's examination, and the 28th. If so, the retention of the name of Robert Winter amongst the diggers, and that of Keyes amongst those made privy afterwards, needs no further explanation.[3] Cromwell once

[1] *Proclamation Book, R.O.*

[2] *G. P. B.* No. 129.

[3] 'The Discourse of the Powder Treason,' published in Bishop Montague's *Works of James I.*, p. 233, only forms part of the original so-called 'King's Book,' which was published anonymously in 1605 (*i.e.*, before March 25, 1606) under the title of *His Majesty's*

adjured the Presbyterians of Edinburgh to believe it possible that they might be mistaken. If Father Gerard would only believe it possible that Salisbury may have been mistaken, he would hardly be so keen to mark conscious deception, where deception is not

Speech in this last Session of Parliament . . . together with a Discourse of the Manner of the Discovery of this late Intended Treason, joined with the Examination of Some of the Prisoners.—Brit. Mus., Press Mark E. 1940, No. 10. In the Preface directed by the Printer to the Reader, the Printer states that he was about to commit the Speech to the press when there came into his hands 'a discourse of this late intended most abominable treason,' which he has added. The King's speech was delivered on November 9, and, if it was to be published, it is not likely to have been long kept back. The discourse consists of four parts—1. An account of the discovery of the plot, and arrest of Fawkes. 2. Fawkes's declaration of the 17th. 3. Winter's confession of the 23rd. 4. An account of the flight and capture of the conspirators. The whole composition shows signs of an early date. Part 1 knows nothing of any names except those of Percy and Johnson *alias* Fawkes, and was probably, therefore, drawn up before the confession of the 9th. At the end it slips off from a statement that Fawkes, having been 'twice or thrice examined when the rack having been only offered and showed unto him, the mask of his Roman fortitude did visibly begin to wear and slide off his face, and then did he begin to confess part of the truth,' into 'and thereafter to open up the whole matter as doth appear by his depositions immediately following.' Then comes the declaration of November 17, with Winter amongst the diggers and Keyes amongst those afterwards made privy. Between Parts 2 and 3 we have the following statement: "And in regard that before this discovery could be ready to go to the press, Thomas Winter, being apprehended and brought to the Tower, made a confession in substance agreeing with this former of Fawkes's, only larger in some circumstances. I have thought good to insert the same likewise in this place, for the further clearing of the matter and greater benefit of the reader." May we not gather from this that the 'discourse' was finally made up for the press on or very soon after the 23rd? Winter, it may be noted, does not mention the name either of his brother or of Keyes.

necessarily to be found. After all, the Government left the names of Winter and Keyes perfectly legible under the pen-strokes drawn across them, and the change they made was at least the erasure of a false statement and the substitution of a true one.

CHAPTER IV.

STRUCTURAL DIFFICULTIES.

From a study of the documentary evidence, I pass to an examination of those structural conditions which Father Gerard pronounces to be fatal to the 'traditional' story. The first step is obviously to ascertain the exact position of Whynniard's house, part of which was rented by Percy. The investigator is, however, considerably assisted by Father Gerard, who has successfully exploded the old belief that this building lay to the south-west of the House of Lords. His argument, which appears to me to be conclusive, runs as follows:—

"That the lodging hired by Percy stood near the south-east corner of the old House of Lords (*i.e.* nearer to the river than that building, and adjacent to, if not adjoining the Prince's Chamber) is shown by the following arguments:—

"1. John Shepherd, servant to Whynniard, gave evidence as to having on a certain occasion seen from the river 'a boat lie close to the pale of Sir Thomas Parry's garden, and men going to and from the water through the back door that leadeth into Mr. Percy, his lodging.—[*Gunpowder Plot Book*, 40, part 2.]

"2. Fawkes, in his examination of November 5, 1605,

speaks of the window in his chamber near the Parliament House towards the water-side.

"3. It is said that when digging their mine the conspirators were troubled by the influx of water from the river, which would be impossible if they were working at the opposite side of the Parliament House." [1]

I think, however, that a still closer identification is possible. On page 80 will be seen a frontage towards the river, marked 'very old walls, remaining in 1795 & 1800,' of which the line corresponds fairly with that of the house in the view given as the frontispiece to this volume.

On part of the site behind it is written 'Very Old House,' and the remainder is said to have been occupied by a garden for many years. It may, however, be gathered from the view that this piece of ground was covered by part of the house in 1799, and I imagine that the 'many years' must have commenced in 1807, when the house was demolished (see view at p. 89). If any doubt remains as to the locality of the front it will be removed by Capon's pencilled note on the door to the left,[2] stating that it led to Parliament Place.[3]

The house marked separately to the right in the plan, as Mrs. Robe's house, 1799, is evidently identical

[1] *Gerard*, App. E., p. 251.

[2] This note is on too small a scale to be reproduced in the frontispiece.

[3] This name is given at a later time to the 'Passage leading to the Parliament Stairs' of Capon's plan, and I have, for convenience sake, referred to it throughout by that name.

with the more modern building in the frontispiece, and therefore does not concern us.

With this comparatively modern plan should be compared the three which follow in succession (pp. 81, 82, 83), respectively dated 1685, 1739, and 1761. They are taken from the Crace Collection of plans in the Print Room of the British Museum, Portfolio xi. Nos. 30, 45, 46.

The first of these three plans differs from the later ones in two important particulars. In the first place, the shaded part indicating buildings is divided by dark lines, and, in the second place, this shaded part covers more ground. I suppose there can be little doubt that the dark lines indicate party walls, and we are thus enabled to understand how it is that, whilst in writing to Parry [1] Salisbury speaks of Percy as having taken a part of Whynniard's house, Percy is spoken of in all the remaining evidence that has reached us as taking a house. Salisbury, no doubt, was thinking of the whole tenement held by Whynniard as a house, whilst others gave that name to such a part of it as could be separately held by a single tenant. The other difference between the plans is less easy to explain. Neither of the later ones show that excrescence towards the river-bank, abutting on its northern side on Cotton Garden, which is so noted a feature in the plan of 1685. At one time I was inclined to think that we had here the 'low room new builded,' that in which Percy at first stored

[1] See p. 22.

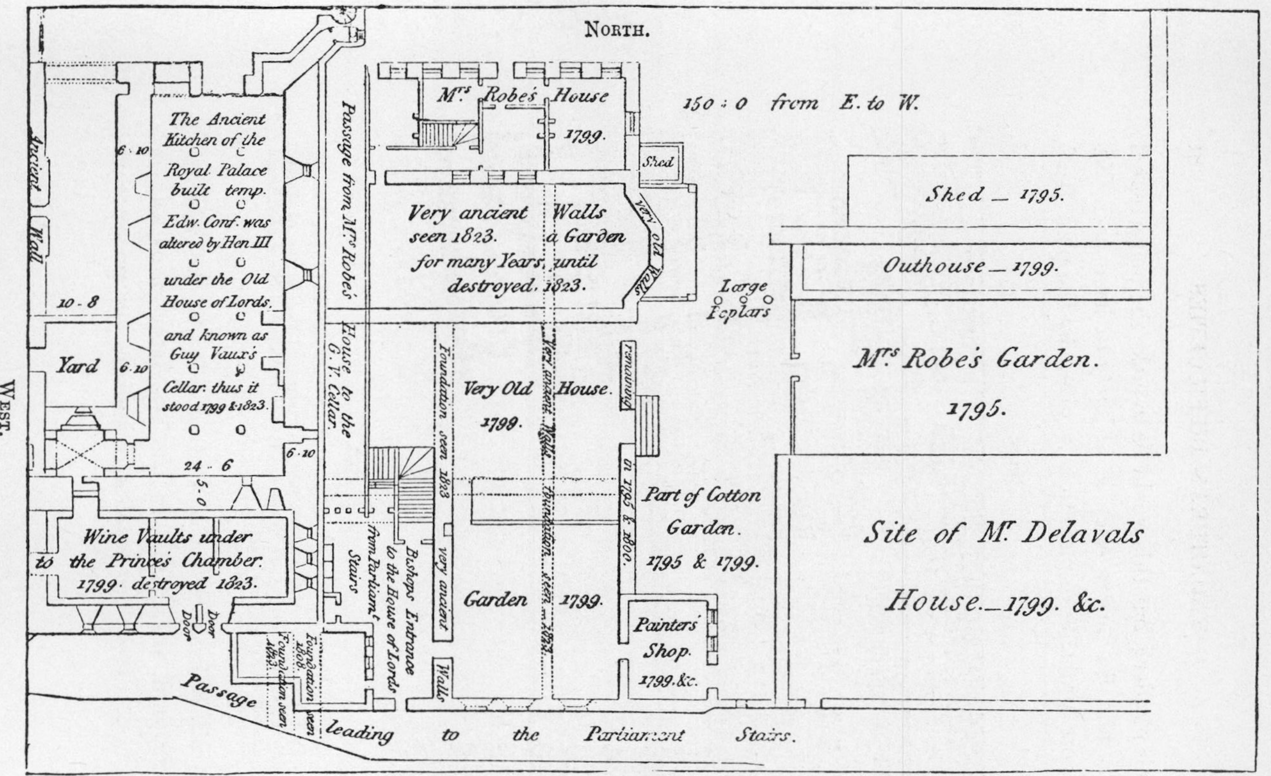

Part of a Plan of the Ancient Palace of Westminster, by the late Mr. William Capon, Measured and Drawn between 1793 and 1823.—*Vetusta Monumenta*, vol. v. The houses at the edge of the river were not in existence in 1605, the ground on which they were built having been reclaimed since that date.

his powder; but this would be to make the house rented by him far larger than it is likely to have been. A more probable explanation is given by the plan itself.

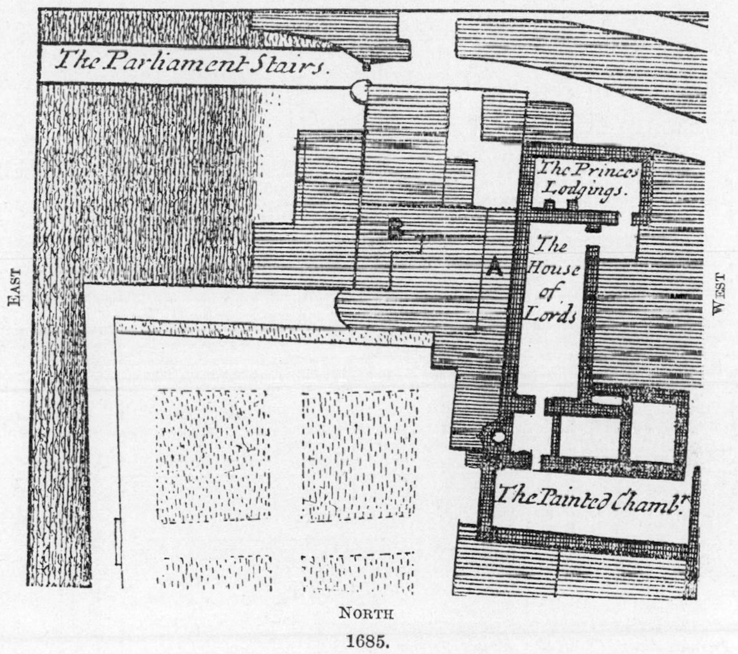

1685.

FROM A PLAN OF PART OF WESTMINSTER, 1685.

A. Probable position of the chamber attached to the House of Lords. B. Probable position of the house leased to Percy. These references are not in the original plan.

It will be seen that the shading includes the internal courtyard, perceptible in the two later plans, and it does not therefore necessarily indicate the presence of buildings. May not the shaded part reaching to the river mean no more than that in 1685 there

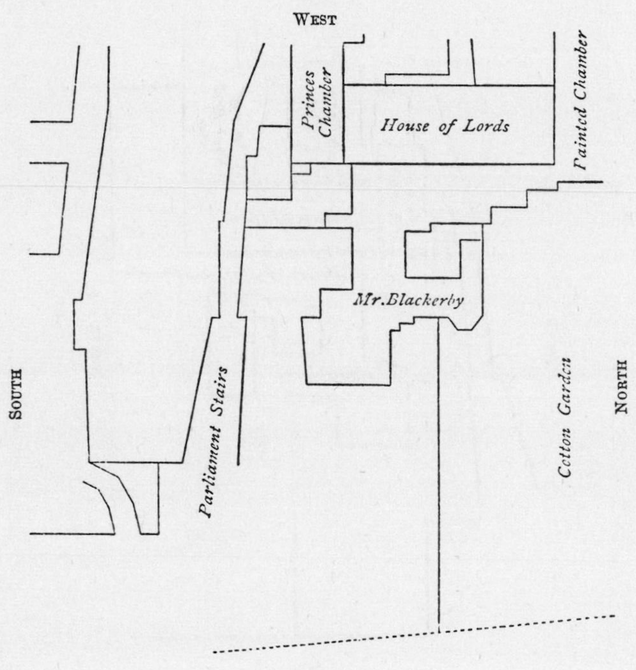

1739.

FROM A PLAN OF PART OF WESTMINSTER, WITH INTENDED IMPROVEMENTS OF THE HOUSES OF LORDS AND COMMONS, BY W. KENT, 1739.

A red line showing the ground set apart by Kent for building is omitted.

was some yard or garden specially attached to the House?

Before giving reasons for selecting any one part of Whynniard's block as that rented from him by Percy,

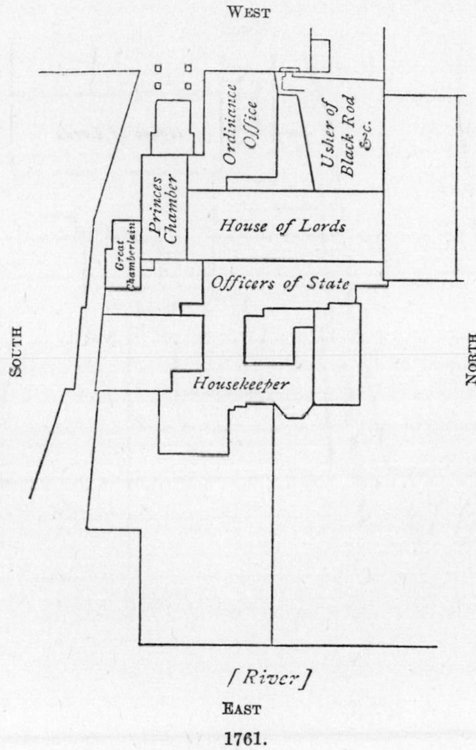

1761.

FROM A PLAN OF WESTMINSTER HALL AND THE HOUSES OF PARLIAMENT AS IT APPEARED IN 1761

Part of this lettering is in pencil in the original plan.

it is necessary to face a difficulty raised by Father Gerard:—

"Neither," he writes, "does the house appear to have been well suited for the purposes for which it was taken.

Speed tells us, and he is confirmed by Bishop Barlow, of Lincoln, that it was let out to tenants only when Parliament was not assembled, and during a session formed part of the premises at the disposal of the Lords, whom it served as a withdrawing room. As this plot was of necessity to take effect during a session, when the place would be in other hands, it is very hard to understand how it was intended that the final and all-important operation should be conducted."[1]

This objection is put still more strongly in a subsequent passage:—

"We have already observed on the nature of the house occupied in Percy's name. If this were, as Speed tells us, and as there is no reason to doubt, at the service of the Peers during a session for a withdrawing-room, and if the session was to begin on November 5, how could Fawkes hope not only to remain in possession, but to carry on his strange proceedings unobserved amid the crowd of lacqueys and officials with whom the opening of the Parliament by the Sovereign must needs have flooded the premises. How was he, unobserved, to get into the fatal 'cellar'?"[2]

It is easy enough to brush away Father Gerard's alleged confirmation by Bishop Barlow,[3] who, writing as he did in the reign of Charles II., carries no weight on such a point. Besides, he did not write a book on the Gunpowder Plot at all. He merely republished, in 1679, an old official narrative of the trial, with an

[1] *Gerard*, p. 62. [2] *Gerard*, pp. 141, 142.

[3] I suppose Thomas Barlow is meant. William Barlow, who was Bishop of Lincoln in the reign of James I., did not write about the plot.

unimportant preface of his own. What Father Gerard quotes here and elsewhere is, however, not even taken from this republication, but from an anonymous pamphlet published in 1678, and reprinted in *The Harleian Miscellany*, iii. 121, which is avowedly a cento made up from earlier writers, and in which the words referred to are doubtless copied directly from Speed.

Speed's own testimony, however, cannot be so lightly dismissed, especially as it is found in the first edition of his *History*, published in 1611, and therefore only six years after the event:—

> "No place," he says, "was held fitter than a certain edifice adjoining the wall of the Parliament House, which served for withdrawing rooms for the assembled Lords, and out of Parliament was at the disposal of the keeper of the place and wardrobe thereunto belonging."[1]

This is quite specific, and unless Speed's evidence can be in any way modified, fully justifies Father Gerard in his contention. Let us, however, turn to the agreement for the house in question:—

> "Memorandum that it is concluded between Thomas Percy of London Esquire and Henry Ferrers of Bordesley Clinton in the County of Warwick Gentleman the xxiiii day of March in the second year of our Sovereign Lord King James.[2]
>
> "That the said Henry hath granted to the said Thomas to enjoy his house in Westminster belonging to the Parliament House, the said Thomas getting the consent of Mr.

[1] Speed's *History*, ed. 1611, p. 891. [2] March 24th, 1604.

Whynniard, and satisfying me, the said Henry, for my charges bestowed thereupon, as shall be thought fit by two indifferent men chosen between us.

"And that he shall also have the other house that Gideon Gibbons dwelleth in, with an assignment of a lease from Mr. Whynniard thereof, satisfying me as aforesaid, and using the now tenant well.

"And the said Thomas hath lent unto me the said Henry twenty pounds, to be allowed upon reckoning or to be repaid again at the will of the said Thomas.

"HENRY FERRERS.

"Sealed and delivered in the presence of
Jo: White and Christopher Symons.[1]"

It is therefore beyond question, on the evidence of this agreement, that Speed was right in connecting with Parliament a house rented by Percy. It is, however, also beyond question, on the evidence of the same agreement, that he also took a second house, of which Whynniard was to give him a lease. The inference that Percy would have been turned out of this second house when Parliament met seems, therefore, to be untenable. Whynniard, it may be observed, had, on March 24, 1602, been appointed, in conjunction with his son, Keeper of the Old Palace,[2] so that the block of buildings concerned, which is within the Old Palace, may very well have been his official residence.

Let us now cast our eyes on the plan on p. 81. We find there a long division of the building running

[1] Copy of the Agreement, *G.P.B.*, No. 1. [2] Pat. 44 Eliz., Part 22.

between the wall of the House of Lords and the back wall of the remainder of the block. It certainly looks as if this must have been the house, or division of a house, belonging to Parliament, and this probability is turned into something like certainty by the two views that now follow, taken from the *Crace Collection*; Views, Portfolio, xv., Nos. 18, 26.

It will be seen that the first of these two views, taken in 1804 (p. 88), shows us a large mullioned window, inside which must have been a room of some considerable length to require so large an opening to admit light, as its breadth must evidently have been limited. Such a room would be out of place in the rambling building we have been examining, but by no means out of place as a chamber or gallery connected with the House of Lords, and capable of serving as a place of meeting for the Commissioners appointed to consider a scheme of union with Scotland. A glance at the view on page 89, which was taken in 1807, when the wall of the House of Lords was being laid bare by the demolition of the houses abutting on it, shows two apertures, a window with a Gothic arch, and an opening with a square head, which may very well have served as a door, whilst the window may have been blocked up. If such a connection with the House of Lords can be established, there seems no reason to doubt that we have the withdrawing room fixed beyond doubt. Father Gerard mentions an old print representing 'the two Houses assembled in the presence of Queen Elizabeth,' and having 'windows on both sides.'[1] Such a print can only refer to a time before the mullioned chamber was in existence, and

East End of the Prince's Chamber.
Published July 1, 1804, by J. T. Smith.

therefore—unless this print, like a subsequent one, was a mere copy of an earlier one still—we have fair

[1] *Gerard*, p. 60, note 1.

VIEWS OF THE EAST SIDE OF THE HOUSE OF LORDS, THE EAST END OF THE PRINCE'S CHAMBER, &C.
TAKEN OCTOBER 8, 1807.

N.B. From the doorway out of which a man is peeping, nearly in the centre of the print, Guy Fawkes was to have made his escape. Published Nov. 4, 1807, by J. T. Smith.

evidence that the large room was not in existence in some year in the reign of Elizabeth, whilst the plan at p. 80 shows that it was in existence in 1685. That it was there in 1605 is not, indeed, to be proved by other evidence than that it manifestly supplies us with the withdrawing room for the Lords and for the Commissioners for the Union of which we hear so much.

That in the early part of the nineteenth century the storey beneath this room was occupied by a passage leading from the court opening on Parliament Place, and Cotton Garden, is shown in the plan at p. 81; and the views at pp. 88, 89, rather indicate that that passage was in existence when the old house, which I call Whynniard's block, was still undemolished. If this was so, we are able to find a place for the 'little entry,' under which, according to Winter, the conspirators worked. This view of the case, too, is borne out by Smith's statement, that 'in the further end of that court,' *i.e.* the court running up from Parliament Place, 'is a doorway, through which, and turning to the left through another doorway, is the immediate way out of the cellar where the powder-plot was intended to take effect.'[1] It seems likely that the whole long space under the withdrawing room was used as a passage, though, on the other hand, the part of what was afterwards a passage may have been

[1] *Smith's Antiquities of Westminster*, p. 39. The question of the number of doors in the cellar will be dealt with hereafter.

blocked by a room, in which case we have the 'low room new builded'—*i.e.* built in some year in Elizabeth's reign—in which the powder was stored.

Having thus fixed the position of the house belonging to Parliament, and shown that it probably consisted of a long room in one storey, we can hardly fail to discover the second house as that marked B in the plan on p. 81, since that house alone combines the conditions of being close to the House of Lords, and having a door and window looking towards the river.

According to Father Gerard, however, the premises occupied by Percy were far too small to make this explanation permissible.

"We learn," he says, "on the unimpeachable evidence of Mrs. Whynniard's servant that the house afforded accommodation only for one person at a time, so that when Percy came there to spend the night, Fawkes, who passed for his man, had to lodge out. This suggests another question. Percy's pretext for laying in so much fuel was that he meant to bring up his wife to live there. But how could this be under such conditions?"[1]

Mrs. Whynniard's servant, however, Roger James, did not use the words here put into his mouth. He said that he had heard from Mrs. Gibbons 'that Mr. Percy hath lain in the said lodging divers times himself, but when he lay there, his man lay abroad, there being but one bed in the said lodging.'

Fawkes, therefore, lodged out when his master came,

[1] *Gerard*, p. 67.

not because there was not a second room in the house, but because there was only one bed. If Mrs. Percy arrived alone she would probably find one bed sufficient for herself and her husband. If she brought any maid-servants with her, beds could be provided for them without much difficulty. Is it not likely that the plan of sending Fawkes out to sleep was contrived with the object of persuading the Whynniards that as matters stood no more than one person could occupy the house at night, and of thus putting them off the scent, at the time when the miners were congregated in it?

A more serious problem is presented by Father Gerard's inquiry 'how proceedings so remarkable' as the digging of the mine could have escaped the notice, not only of the Government, but of the entire neighbourhood.

"This," he continues, "it must be remembered, was most populous. There were people living in the very building a part of which sheltered the conspirators. Around were thickly clustered the dwellings of the Keeper of the Wardrobe, auditors and tellers of the Exchequer, and other such officials. There were tradespeople and workmen constantly employed close to the spot where the work was going on; while the public character of the place makes it impossible to suppose that tenants such as Percy and his friends, who were little better than lodgers, could claim the exclusive use of anything beyond the rooms they rented—even when allowed the use of them—or could shut against the neighbours and visitors in general the precincts of so frequented a spot." [1]

[1] *Gerard*, p. 65.

To this is added the following footnote:—

"The buildings of the dissolved College of St. Stephen, comprising those around the House of Lords, were granted by Edward VI. to Sir Ralph Lane. They reverted to the Crown under Elizabeth, and were appropriated as residences for the auditors and tellers of the Exchequer. The locality became so populous that in 1606 it was forbidden to erect more houses."

This statement is reinforced by a conjectural view of the neighbourhood founded on the 'best authorities' by Mr. H. W. Brewer.[1] Mr. Brewer who has since kindly examined with me the drawings and plans in the Crace Collection, on which I rely, has, I think, been misled by those early semi-pictorial maps, which, though they may be relied on for larger buildings, such as the House of Lords or St. Stephen's Chapel, are very imaginative in their treatment of private houses. In any case I deny the existence of the two large houses placed by him between what I infer to have been Whynniard's house and the river side.

The history of the land between the wall of the old palace on which stood the river front of Whynniard's house, and the bank of the Thames, can be traced with tolerable accuracy. It formed part of a larger estate, formerly the property of the dissolved chapel of St. Stephen, granted by Edward VI. to Sir Ralph Fane;[2] Father Gerard's Sir Ralph Lane being a misprint or a mistake. Fane, however, was hanged

[1] P. 56.

[2] Pat. 4 Edw. *VI.*. Part 9.

shortly afterwards, and the estate, reverting to the Crown, was re-granted to Sir John Gates.[1] Again reverting to the Crown, it was dealt with in separate portions, and the part on which the Exchequer officers' residences was built was to the north of Cotton Garden, and being quite out of earshot of Whynniard's house, need not concern us here. In 1588, the Queen granted to John Whynniard, then an officer of the Wardrobe, a lease of several parcels of ground for thirty years.[2] Some of these were near Whitehall, others to the south of Parliament Stairs. The only one which concerns us is a piece of land lying between the wall of the Old Palace, on which the river-front of Whynniard's house was built, and the Thames. In 1600 the reversion was granted to two men named Evershed and Holland, who immediately sold it to Whynniard, thus constituting him the owner of the land in perpetuity. In the deed conveying it to him, this portion is styled :—

"All that piece of waste land lying there right against the said piece, and lieth and is without the said stone wall, that is to say between the said passage or entry of the said Parliament House[3] on the north part, and abutteth upon the said stone wall which compasseth the said Old Palace towards the West, and upon the Thames aforesaid towards the East, and continueth at length between the passage aforesaid and the sluice coming from the said Parliament House, seventy-five foot."[4]

[1] Pat. 6 Edw. *VI.*, Part 5.

[2] Pat. 30 Eliz., Part 10.

[3] Parliament Place.

[4] Assignment, July 17, 42 Eliz., *Land Revenue Records Office*,

On this piece of waste land I place the garden mentioned in connection with the house rented by Percy. This is far more probable than it was where Mr. Brewer has placed it, in the narrow court which leads from Parliament Place to the other side of Percy's house, and ends by the side of the Prince's Chamber. If this arrangement be accepted, it gets rid of the alleged populousness of neighbourhood. No doubt people flocked up and down from Parliament Stairs, but they would be excluded from the garden on the river side, and with few exceptions would pass on without turning to the right into the court. Nobody who had not business with Percy himself or with his neighbour on the south[1] would be likely to approach Percy's door. As far as that side of the house was concerned, it would be difficult to find a more secluded dwelling. The Thames was then 'the silent highway' of London, and the sight of a barge unloading before the back door of a house can have been no more surprising than the sight of a gondola moored to the steps of a palace on a canal in Venice. John Shepherd, for instance, was not startled by the sight :—

Memorandum that John Shepherd servant to the said

Inrolments v. fol. 104. I have been unable to trac Whynniard's tenure of the house I have assigned to him. It was within the Old Palace, and was probably the official residence of its keeper . Whynniard was appointed Keeper of the Old Palace in 1602 Pat. 44 Eliz., Part 22.

[1] See plan at p. 81. Was this the baker in whose house Catesby tried in vain to secure a room ?—'Bates's Confession, Dec. 4, 1605 '; *G. P. B.* No. 145.

Mr. Whynniard, saith that the fourth of September last being Wednesday before the Queen's Majesty removed from Windsor to Hampton Court,[1] he being taken suddenly sick, and therefore sent away to London, and coming late to lie at the Queen's Bridge,[2] the tide being high, he saw a boat lie close by the pale of Sir Thomas Parry's garden [3] and men going to and fro the water through the back door that leadeth into Mr. Percy's lodging, which he doth now bethink himself of, though then, being sick and late, he did not regard it.[4]

It thus appears that this final supply of powder was carried in at night, and by a way through the garden—not by the more frequented Parliament Stairs.

The story of the mine, no doubt, presents some difficulties which, though by no means insuperable, cannot be solved with absolute certainty without more information than we possess at present. We may, I think, dismiss the suggestion of the Edinburgh Reviewer that the conspirators may have dug straight down instead of making a tunnel, both because even bunglers could hardly have occupied a fortnight in digging a pit a few feet deep, and because their words about reaching the wall at the end of the fortnight would, on this hypothesis, have no meaning. Thomas Winter's statement is that he and his comrades

[1] Whynniard was Keeper of the Wardrobe at Hampton Court, which would account for his servant being concerned in the Queen's removal.

[2] Otherwise Parliament Stairs.

[3] I suspect that this was what was afterwards known as Cotton Garden. I have been unable to trace the date at which it was conveyed to Sir Robert Cotton.

[4] *G. P. B.* No. 40.

'wrought under a little entry to the wall of the Parliament House.'[1] The little entry, as I have already argued,[2] must be the covered passage under the withdrawing room; a tunnel leading from the cellar of Percy's house would be about seven or eight feet long. The main difficulty at the commencement of the work would be to get through the wall of Percy's house, and this, it may be noticed, neither Fawkes nor Winter speak of, though they are very positive as to the difficulties presented by the wall of the House of Lords. If, indeed, the wall on this side of Percy's house was, as may with great probability be conjectured, built of brick, as the river front undoubtedly was,[3] the difficulty cannot have been great, as I have been informed by Mr. Henry Ward[4] that the brick used in those days was, both from its composition and from the method in which it was dried, far softer than that employed in building at present. We may, therefore, fairly start our miners in the cellar of their own house with a soft brick wall to penetrate, and a tunnel afterwards to construct, having wood ready to prop up the earth, and appropriate implements to carry out their undertaking.[5]

[1] See p. 63. [2] See p. 90.

[3] This we know from Capon's pencilled notes to the sketch in the frontispiece.

[4] The late Chairman of the Works Department of the London County Council; than whom no man is better qualified to speak on such matters.

[5] There are indeed old walls marked in Capon's plan beneath the ground, but we do not know of what substance they were composed or how near the surface they came.

Here, however, Father Gerard waves us back:—

"It is not easy," he writes, "to understand how these amateurs contrived to do so much without a catastrophe. To make a tunnel through soft earth is a very delicate operation, replete with unknown difficulties. To shore up the roof and sides there must, moreover, have been required a large quantity of the 'framed timber' [1] of which Speed tells us, and the provision and importation of this must have been almost as hard to keep dark as the exportation of the earth and stones. A still more critical operation is that of meddling with the foundations of a house—especially of an old and heavy structure—which a professional craftsman would not venture upon except with extreme care, and the employment of many precautions of which these light-hearted adventurers knew nothing. Yet, recklessly breaking their way out of one building, and to a large extent into another, they appear to have occasioned neither crack nor settlement in either." [2]

I have already dealt with the problem of bringing in articles by night, and of getting through Percy's wall. For the rest, Father Gerard forgets that though six of the seven miners were amateurs, the seventh was not. Fawkes had been eight years in the service of the Archdukes in the Low Countries, and to soldiers on either side the war in the Low Countries offered the most complete school of military mining then to be found in the world. Though every soldier was not an engineer, he could not fail to be

[1] Speed, no doubt, rested this assertion on Winter's evidence that 'we underpropped it, as we went, with wood.' (See p. 64.)

[2] *Gerard*, pp. 66, 67.

in the way of hearing about, if not of actually witnessing, feats of engineering skill, of which the object was not merely to undermine fortifications with tunnels of far greater length than can have been required by the conspirators, but to conduct the operation as quietly as possible. It must surely have been the habit of these engineers to use other implements than the noisy pick of the modern workman.[1] Fawkes, indeed, speaks of himself merely as a watcher whilst others worked. But he was a modest man, and there can be no reasonable doubt that he directed the operations.

When the main wall was attacked after Christmas the conditions were somewhat altered. The miners, indeed, may still have been able to avoid the use of picks, and to employ drills and crowbars, but some noise they must necessarily have made. Yet the chances of their being overheard were very slight. Having taken the precaution to hire the long withdrawing room and the passage or passage-room beneath it, the sounds made on the lower part of the main wall could not very well reach the ears of the tenants of the other houses in Whynniard's block. The only question is whether there was any one likely to hear them in the so-called 'cellar' underneath the House of Lords, beneath which, again, they intended to deposit their

[1] See the remarks of the Edinburgh Reviewer on the ease with which Baron Trenck executed a far harder piece of work without being discovered for a considerable time.

store of powder. What that chamber was had best be told in Father Gerard's own words:—

"The old House of Lords,"[1] he writes, "was a chamber occupying the first floor of a building which stood about fifty yards from the left bank of the Thames,[2] to which it was parallel, the stream at this point running about due north. Beneath the Peers' Chamber on the ground floor was a large room, which plays an important part in our history. This had originally served as the palace kitchen, and, though commonly described as a 'cellar' or a 'vault, was in reality neither, for it stood on the level of the ground outside, and had a flat ceiling formed by the beams which supported the flooring of the Lords apartment above. It ran beneath the said Peers' Chamber from end to end, and measured seventy-seven feet in length by twenty-four feet four inches in width.

"At either end the building abutted upon another running transversely to it; that on the north being the 'Painted Chamber,' probably erected by Edward the Confessor, and that on the south the 'Prince's Chamber,' assigned by its architectural features to the reign of Henry III. The former served as a place of conference for Lords and Commons, the latter as the robing-room of the Lords. The royal throne stood at the south end of the House, near the Prince's Chamber."[3]

According to the story told by Fawkes this place was let to Mrs. Skinner by Whynniard to store her

[1] Used as such, Father Gerard notes, till the Union with Ireland in 1800.

[2] This was true of the general line of the bank, but, as will be seen at pp. 81, 83, there was a kind of dock which brought the water within about thirty yards of the house.

[3] *Gerard*, pp. 59, 60.

coals in. In an early draft of the narrative usually known as the 'King's Book,'[1] we are told that there was 'some stuff of the King's which lay in part of a cellar under those rooms'—*i.e.* the House of Lords, and 'that Whynniard had let out some part of a room directly under the Parliament chamber to one that used it for a cellar.' This statement is virtually repeated in the 'King's Book' itself, where Whynniard is said to have stated 'that Thomas Percy had hired both the house and part of the cellar or vault under the same.'[2] That part was so let is highly probable, as the internal length of the old kitchen was about seventy-seven feet, and it would therefore be far too large for the occupation of a single coalmonger. We must thus imagine the so-called vault divided into two portions, probably with a partition cutting off one from the other. If, therefore, the conspirators restricted their operations to the night-time, there was little danger of their being overheard. There was not much likelihood either that Whynniard would get out of bed to visit the tapestry or whatever the stuff belonging to the King may have been, or that Mrs. Skinner would want to examine her coal-sacks whilst her customers were asleep. The only risk was from some belated visitor coming up the quiet court leading from Parliament Place to make his way to one of the houses in Whyn-

[1] *G. P. B.* No. 129.

[2] This is clearly a slip. The cellar was not under the house hired by Percy.

niard's block. Against this, however, the plotters were secured by the watchfulness of Fawkes.

The precautions taken by the conspirators did not render their task easier. It was in the second fortnight, beginning after the middle of January, when the hard work of getting through the strong and broad foundation of the House of Lords tried their muscles and their patience, that they swore in Christopher Wright, and brought over Keyes from Lambeth together with the powder which they now stored in 'a low room new-builded.'[1] After a fortnight's work. reaching to Candlemas (Feb. 2), they had burrowed through about four feet six inches into the wall, after which they again gave over working.[2] Some time in the latter part of March they returned to their operations, but they had scarcely commenced when they found out that it would be possible for them to gain possession of a locality more suited to their wants, and they there-

[1] For its possible situation see p. 91; or it may have been erected in the courtyard shown in the plans at pp. 82, 83.

[2] See pp. 34, 65. The difficulty of measuring the thickness of the wall was not so great as Father Gerard fancies. In 1678 Sir Christopher Wren reported that 'the walls are seven feet thick below' (*Hist. MSS.* Com. Report XI. App. ii. p. 17). As he did not dig below the surface this must mean that they were seven feet thick at the level of the floor of the so-called cellar, and this measurement must have been known to the conspirators after they had access to it. I am informed that in the case of a heavy wall, especially when it is built on light soil, as was the case here, the foundations are always constructed to be broader than the wall itself. The diggers, observing the angle of the face they attacked, might roughly calculate that a foot on each side might be added, thus reaching the nine feet.

fore abandoned the project of the mine as no longer necessary.[1]

Before passing from the story of the mine, the more important of Father Gerard's criticisms require an answer. How, he asks, could the conspirators have got rid of such a mass of earth and stones without exciting attention?[2] Fawkes, indeed, says that 'the day before Christmas having a mass of earth that came out of the mine, they carried it into the garden of the said house.' Then Goodman declares that he saw it,[3] but, even if we assume that his memory did not play him false, it is impossible that the whole of the produce of the first fortnight's diggings should be disposed of in this way. The shortest length that can be ascribed to the mine before the wall was reached is eight feet, and if we allow five feet for height and depth we have 200 cubical

[1] Father Gerard (p. 64, note 2) writes: "There is, as usual, hopeless confusion between the two witnesses upon whom, as will be seen, we wholly depend for this portion of the story. Fawkes (November 17, 1605) makes the mining operations terminate at Candlemas, and Winter (November 23) says that they went on to 'near Easter' (March 31). The date of the hiring the 'cellar' was about Lady Day (March 25)." I can see no contradiction. The resumption of work for a third time in March was, from Winter's mode of referring to it, evidently for a very short time. "And," he says, 'near to Easter, as we wrought the third time, opportunity was given to hire the cellar." Fawkes, though less clear and full, implicitly says much the same thing. He says that 'about Candlemas we had wrought the wall half through,' and then goes on to describe how he stood sentinel, &c. Then at the beginning of another paragraph we have "As they were working upon the wall they heard a rushing in a cellar, &c." Fawkes gives no dates, but he says nothing to contradict the third working spoken of by Winter.

[2] *Gerard*, pp. 65, 66.

[3] *Goodman*, i. 104.

feet, or a mass more than six feet every way, besides the stones coming out of the wall after Christmas. Some of the earth may have been, as Fawkes said, spread over the garden beds, but the greater part of it must have been disposed of in some other way. Is it so very difficult to surmise what that was? The nights were long and dark, and the river was very close.

We are further asked to explain how it was that, if there was really a mine, the Government did not find it out for some days after the arrest of Fawkes. Why should they? The only point at which it was accessible was at its entrance in Percy's own cellar, and it is an insult to the sharp wits of the plotters, to suppose that they did not close it up as soon as the project of the mine was abandoned. All that would be needed, if the head of the mine descended, as it probably did, would be the relaying of a couple or so of flagstones. How careful the plotters were of wiping out all traces of their work, is shown by the evidence of Whynniard's servant, Roger James, who says that about Midsummer 1605, Percy, appearing to pay his quarter's rent, 'agreed with one York, a carpenter in Westminster, for the repairing of his lodging,' adding 'that he would send his man to pay the carpenter for the work he was to do.' [1] Either

[1] *G. P. B.* No. 40. Father Gerard (p. 142) says that we learn on the unimpeachable testimony of Mrs. Whynniard, the landlady, that Fawkes not only paid the last instalment of rent on Sunday, November 3, but on the following day, the day immediately preceding the intended explosion, had carpenters and other work folk in the house for mending and repairing thereof (*G. P. B.* No 39). "To say

the mine had no existence, or all traces of it must have been effectually removed before a carpenter was allowed to range the house in the absence of both Percy and Fawkes. I must leave it to my readers to decide which alternative they prefer.

According to the usually received story, the conspirators, hearing a rustling above their heads, imagined that their enterprise had been discovered, but having sent Fawkes to ascertain the cause of the noise, they learnt that Mrs. Skinner (afterwards Mrs. Bright) was selling coals, and having also ascertained that she was willing to give up her tenancy to them for a consideration, they applied to Whynniard—from whom the so-called 'cellar' was leased—through his wife, and obtained a transfer of the premises to Percy. All that remained was to convey the powder from the house to the 'cellar,' and after covering it with billets and faggots, to wait quietly till Parliament met.

Father Gerard's first objection to this is, that whilst they were mining, 'ridiculous as is the supposition, the conspirators appear to have been ignorant of the existence of the "cellar," and to have fancied that they were

nothing of the wonderful honesty of paying rent under the circumstances, what was the sense of putting a house in repair upon Monday, which on Tuesday was to be blown to atoms?" The rent having fallen due at Michaelmas, is it not probable that it was paid in November to avoid legal proceedings, which might at least have drawn attention to the occupier of the house. As to the rest, the 'unimpeachable testimony' is that—not of Mrs. Whynniard, but of Roger James (*G. P. B.* No. 40), who says that the carpenter came in about Midsummer, not on November 4.

working their way immediately beneath the Chamber of Peers.' The supposition would be ridiculous enough if it were not a figment of Father Gerard's own brain. He relies on what he calls 'Barlow's Gunpowder Treason,' [1] published in 1678, and on a remark made by Tierney in 1841, adding that it is 'obviously implied' by Fawkes and Winter. What Fawkes says on November 17 is:—

"As they were working upon the wall, they heard a rushing in a cellar of removing of coals; whereupon we feared we had been discovered, and they sent me to go to the cellar, who finding that the coals were a selling, and that the cellar was to be let, viewing the commodity thereof for our purpose, Percy went and hired the same for yearly rent." [2]

What Winter says is that, 'near to Easter . . . opportunity was given to hire the cellar, in which we resolved to lay the powder and leave the mine.' What single word is there here about the conspirators thinking that there was no storey intervening between the foundation and the House of Lords? The mere fact of Percy having been in the house close to the passage from which there was an opening closed only by a grating into the 'cellar' itself, [3] would negative the impossible supposition. Father Gerard, however, adds that Mrs. Whynniard tells us that the cellar was not to let, and that Bright, *i.e.* Mrs. Skinner, had not the disposal of the lease, but one Skinner, and that Percy 'laboured very earnestly before he succeeded in obtaining it.'

[1] *Gerard*, p. 69. [2] *G. P. B.* No. 101. [3] See p. 108.

What Mrs. Whynniard says is that the cellar had been already let, and that her husband had not the disposal of it. Percy then 'intreated that if he could get Mrs. Skinner's good-will therein, they would then be contented to let him have it, whereto they granted it.'[1] Is not this exactly what one might expect to happen on an application for a lease held by a tenant who proves willing to remove?

Father Gerard proceeds to raise difficulties from the structural nature of the cellar itself. Mr. William Capon, he says, examined the foundations of the House of Lords when it was removed in 1823, and did not discover the hole which the conspirators were alleged to have made. His own statement, however, printed in the fifth volume of *Vetusta Monumenta*,[2] says nothing about the foundations; and besides, as Father Gerard has shown, he had a totally erroneous theory of the place whence he supposes the conspirators to have had access to the 'cellar.' Nothing—as I have learnt by experience—is so likely as a false theory to blind the eyes to existing evidence.

Then we have remarks upon the mode of communication between Percy's house and the cellar. Father Gerard tells us that:—

"Fawkes says (November 6th, 1605) that about the middle of Lent[3] of that year, Percy caused 'a new door' to

[1] *G. P. B.* No. 39. [2] *Gerard*, p. 87.

[3] Here is another 'discrepancy,' which Father Gerard has not noticed. As the 'cellar' was not taken till a little before Easter,

be made into it, that he might have a nearer way out of his own house into the cellar.

"This seems to imply that Percy took the cellar for his firewood when there was no convenient communication between it and his house. Moreover, it is not very easy to understand how a tenant—under such conditions as his—was allowed at discretion to knock doors through the walls of a royal palace. Neither did the landlady say anything of this door-making, when detailing what she knew of Percy's proceedings."

Without perceiving it, Father Gerard proceeds to dispose of the objection he had raised.

"In some notes of Sir E. Coke, it is said 'The powder was first brought into Percy's house, and lay there in a low room new built, and could not have been conveyed into the cellar but that all the street must have seen it; and therefore he caused a new door out of his house into the cellar to be made, where before there had been a grate of iron." [1]

To Father Gerard this 'looks very like an afterthought.' Considering, however, that every word except the part about the grating is based on evidence which has reached us, it looks to me very like the truth. It is, indeed, useless to attempt to reconcile the position of the doors opening out of the 'cellar' apparently indicated on Capon's plan (p. 80) with those given in

Percy could not make a door into it about the middle of Lent. My solution is, that in his second examination, on November 6th, Fawkes was trying to conceal the existence of the mine, in order that he might not betray the miners, and therefore antedated the making of the door. See p. 25.

[1] *Gerard*, p. 88.

Four walls of the so-called cellar under the House of Lords. From Smith's *Antiquities of Westminster*, p. 39.

Smith's views (p. 109) of the four walls taken from the inside of the cellar, and I therefore conclude that the apertures shown in the former are really those of the House of Lords on the upper storey, a conjecture which is supported by the insertion of a flight of steps, which would lead nowhere if the whole plan was intended to record merely the features of the lower level. In any case, Smith's illustration shows three entrances —one through the north wall which I have marked A, another with a triangular head near the north end of the east wall marked B, and a third with a square head near the south end of the same wall marked C. The first of these would naturally be used by Mrs. Skinner, as it opened on a passage leading westwards, and we know that she lived in King Street; the second would be used by Whynniard, whilst, either he or some predecessor might very well have put up a grating at the third to keep out thieves. That third aperture was, however, just opposite Percy's house, and when he hired Mrs. Skinner's part of the 'cellar,' he would necessarily wish to have it open and a door substituted for the grating. There was no question of knocking about the walls of a royal palace in the matter. If he had not that door opened he must either use Whynniard's, of which Whynniard presumably wished to keep the key, or go round by Parliament Place to reach the one hitherto used by Mrs. Skinner. It is true that, if the north door was really the one used by Mrs. Skinner, it necessitates the conclusion that there was no insurmountable barrier between Whynniard's part of the cellar, and that afterwards used by Percy. Moreover, it is almost certainly shown that this was the case by the ease with which the searchers got into Percy's part of the cellar on the night of November 4th, though entering by another door. In this case the conspirators must have been content with the strong probability that whenever their landlord came into his end of the 'cellar,' he would not come further to pull about the pile of wood with which their powder barrels were covered. On the other hand, the entrances knocked in blocked-up arches may not have been the same in 1605 and in 1807. At all events, the square-headed aperture in Smith's view agrees so well with that in the view at p. 89, that it can be accepted without doubt as the one in which Percy's new door was substituted for a grating, and which led out of the covered passage opening from the court leading from Parliament Place.

Though it is possible that Whynniard might, if he chose, come into the plotters' 'cellar,' we are under no compulsion to accept Father Gerard's assertion that Winter declared 'that the confederates so arranged as to leave the cellar free for all to enter who would.' [1] "It is stated," writes Father Gerard, in another place, "in Winter's long declaration on this subject, that the barrels were thus completely hidden 'because we might have the house free to suffer anyone to enter that would,' and we find it mentioned by various writers, subsequently,

[1] *Gerard*, p. 89.

that free ingress was actually allowed to the public."[1] As the subsequent writers appear to be an anonymous writer, who wrote on *The Gunpowder Plot* under the pseudonym of L., in 1805, and Hugh F. Martyndale, who wrote *A Familiar Analysis of the Calendar of the Church of England* in 1830, I am unable to take them very seriously. The extraordinary thing is that Father Gerard does not see that his quotation from Winter is fatal to his argument. Winter says that Fawkes covered the powder in the cellar 'because we might have the house free to suffer anyone to enter that would.[2] The cellar was not part of the house; and, although the words are not entirely free from ambiguity, the more reasonable interpretation is that Fawkes disposed of the powder in the cellar, in order that visitors might be freely admitted into the house. Winter, in fact, makes no direct statement that the powder was moved, and it is therefore fair to take this removal as included in what he says about the faggots.

As for the quantity of the gunpowder used, the opinion of the writer discussed in the *Edinburgh Review* (January, 1897), appears reasonable enough:—

"Apart from the hearsay reports, Father Gerard seems to base his computations on the statement that a barrel of gunpowder contained 400 pounds. This is an error. The barrel of gunpowder contained 100 pounds;[3] the last, which is rightly given at 2,400 pounds, contained twenty-four

[1] *Gerard*, p. 74. [2] See p. 66.

[3] See the table in *State Papers relating to the Defeat of the Spanish Armada*, ed. by Prof. Laughton for the Navy Records Society, i. 339.

barrels. The quantity of powder stored in the cellar is repeatedly said, both in the depositions and the indictment to have been thirty-six barrels—that is, a last and a half, or about one ton twelve hundredweight; and this agrees very exactly with the valuation of the powder at 200*l.* In 1588, the cost of a barrel of 100 pounds was 5*l.* But to carry, and move, and stow, a ton and a half in small portable barrels is a very different thing from the task on which Father Gerard dwells of moving and hiding, not only the large barrels of 400 pounds, but also the hogsheads that were spoken of."[1]

I will merely add that Father Gerard's surprise that the disposal of so large a mass of powder is not to be traced is the less justifiable, as the Ordnance accounts of the stores in the Tower have been very irregularly preserved, those for the years with which we are concerned being missing.

Having thus, I hope, shown that the traditional account of the mine and the cellar are consistent with the documentary and structural evidence, I pass to the question of the accuracy of the alleged discovery of the conspiracy.

[1] *Edinburgh Review*, January 1897, p. 200.

CHAPTER V

THE DISCOVERY

In one way the evidence on the discovery of the plot differs from that on the plot itself. The latter is straightforward and simple, its discrepancies, where there are any, being reducible to the varying amount of the knowledge of the Government. The same cannot be said of the evidence relating to the mode in which the plot was discovered. If we accept the traditional story that its discovery was owing to the extraordinary letter brought to Monteagle at Hoxton, there are disturbing elements in the case. In the first place, the Commissioners would probably wish to conceal any mystery connected with the delivery of the letter, if it were only for the sake of Monteagle, to whom they owed so much; and, in the second place, when they had once committed themselves to the theory that the King had discovered the sense of the letter by a sort of Divine inspiration, there could not fail to be a certain amount of shuffling to make this view square with the actual facts. Other causes of hesitancy to set forth the full truth there may have been, but these two were undeniably there.

Father Gerard, however, bars the way to the immediate discussion of these points by a theory which he has indeed adopted from others, but which he has made his own by the fulness with which he has treated it. He holds that Salisbury knew of the plot long before the incident of the letter occurred, a view which is by no means inconsistent with the belief that the plot itself was genuine, and, it may be added, is far less injurious to Salisbury's character than the supposition that he had either partially or wholly invented the plot itself. If the latter charge could have been sustained Salisbury would have to be ranked amongst the most infamous ministers known to history. If all that can be said of him is that he kept silence longer than we should have expected, we may feel curious as to his motives, or question his prudence, but we shall have no reason to doubt his morality.

Father Gerard, having convinced himself that in all probability the Government, or, at least Salisbury, had long had a secret agent amongst the plotters, fixes his suspicions primarily on Percy. Beginning by an attack on Percy's moral character, he writes as follows:—

"It unfortunately appears that, all the time, this zealous convert was a bigamist, having one wife living in the capital and another in the provinces. When his name was published in connection with the Plot, the magistrates of London arrested the one and those of Warwickshire the other, alike reporting to the secretary what they had done, as may be seen in the State Paper Office."[1]

The papers in the Public Record Office here referred to prove nothing of the sort. On November 5 Justice Grange writes to Salisbury that Percy had a house in Holborne 'where his wife is at this instant. She saith her husband liveth not with her, but being attendant on the Right Honourable the Earl of Northumberland, liveth and lodgeth as she supposeth with him. She hath not seen him since Midsummer.[2] She liveth very private and teacheth children. I have caused some to watch the house, as also to guard her until your Honour's pleasure be further known.'[3] There is, however, nothing to show that Salisbury did not within a couple of hours direct that she should be set free, as she had evidently nothing to tell ; nor is there anything here inconsistent with her having been arrested in Warwickshire on the 12th, especially as she was apprehended in the house of John Wright,[4] her brother. What is more likely than that, when the terrible catastrophe befell the poor woman, she should have travelled down to seek refuge in her brother's house, where she might perchance hear some tidings of her husband? It is adding a new terror to matrimony to suggest that a man is liable to be charged with

[1] *Gerard*, p. 148.

[2] We know that Percy visited the house at Westminster at Midsummer. See p. 104.

[3] Grange to Salisbury, Nov. 5.—*G. P. B.* No. 15.

[4] Justices of Warwickshire to Salisbury, Nov. 12.—*Ib.* No. 75.

bigamy because his wife is seen in London one day and in Warwickshire a week afterwards.

The fact probably is that Father Gerard received the suggestion from Goodman, whose belief that Percy was a bigamist rested on information derived from some lady who may very well have been as hardened a gossip as he was himself.[1] His own attempt to bolster up the story by further evidence can hardly be reckoned conclusive.

In any case the question of Percy's morality is quite irrelevant. It is more to the purpose when Father Gerard quotes Goodman as asserting that Percy had been a frequent visitor to Salisbury's house by night.[2]

"Sir Francis Moore," he tells us, ". . . being the lord keeper Egerton's favourite, and having some occasion of business with him at twelve of the clock at night, and going then homeward from York House to the Middle Temple at two, several times he met Mr. Percy, coming out of that great statesman's house, and wondered what his business should be there."[3]

There are many ways in which the conclusion that Percy went to tell tales may be avoided. In the days of James I., the streets of London were inconceivably dark to the man who at the present day is accustomed to gas and electricity. Not even lanterns were permanently hung out for many a year to come. Except when the moon was shining, the only light was

[1] *Goodman*, i. 102. [2] *Gerard*, p. 151. [3] *Goodman*, i. 105.

a lantern carried in the hand, and by the light of either it would be easy to mistake the features of any one coming out from a door way. Yet even if Moore's evidence be accepted, the inference that Percy betrayed the plot to Salisbury is not by any means a necessary one. Percy may, as the Edinburgh Reviewer suggests, have been employed by Northumberland. Nor does Father Gerard recognise that it was clearly Percy's business to place his connection with the Court as much in evidence as possible. The more it was known that he was trusted by Northumberland, and even by Salisbury, the less people were likely to ask awkward questions as to his reasons for taking a house at Westminster. In 1654 a Royalist gentleman arriving from the Continent to take part in an insurrection against the Protector, went straight to Cromwell's Court in order to disarm suspicion. Why may not Percy have acted in a similar way in 1605? All that we know of Percy's character militates against the supposition that he was a man to play the dastardly part of an informer.

Other pieces of evidence against Percy may be dismissed with equal assurance. We are told, for instance,[1] that Salisbury found a difficulty in tracing Percy's movements before the day on which Parliament was to have been blown up; whereas, ten days before, the same Percy had received a pass issued by the Commissioners of the North, as posting to court for the

[1] *Gerard*, p. 152.

King's especial service. The order, however, is signed, not by the Commissioners of the North as a body, but by two of their number, and was dated at Seaton Delaval in Northumberland.[1] As Percy's business is known to have been the bringing up the Earl of Northumberland's rents, and he might have pleaded that it was his duty to be in his place as Gentleman Pensioner at the meeting of Parliament, two gentlemen living within hail of Alnwick were likely enough to stretch a point in favour of the servant of the great earl. In any case it was most unlikely that they should have thought it necessary to acquaint the Secretary of State with the terms in which a posting order had been couched.

The supposition that Salisbury sent secret orders to the sheriff of Worcestershire not to take Percy alive is sufficiently disposed of, as the Edinburgh Reviewer has remarked, by Sheriff Walsh's own letter, and by the extreme improbability that if Salisbury had known Percy to have been a government spy he would have calculated on his being such a lunatic as to join the other conspirators in their flight, apparently for the mere pleasure of getting himself shot.[2] It may be

[1] Warrant, Feb. 8; Commission, Feb. 21; Pass, Oct. 25, 1605.—*S. P. Dom.*, xii. 65; Docquet Book, 1605; *S. P. Dom.*, xv. 106.

[2] To the theory that Salisbury wanted inconvenient witnesses disposed of, because the man who shot Percy and Catesby got a pension of two shillings a day, I reply that the Government was more afraid of a rebellion than of testimony. At all events, 2*s.* at that time was certainly not worth 1*l.* now, as Father Gerard assumes here, and in other passages of his book. It is usual to estimate the value of money as being about four or five times as much

added that it is hard to imagine how Salisbury could know beforehand in what county the rebels would be taken, and consequently to what sheriff he should address his compromising communication. As to the suggestion that there was something hidden behind the failure of the King's messenger to reach the sheriff with orders to avoid killing the chief conspirators, on the ground that 'the distance to be covered was about 112 miles, and there were three days to do it in, for not till November 8 were the fugitives surrounded,' it may fairly be answered, in the first place, that the whereabouts of the conspirators was not known at Westminster till the Proclamation for their arrest was issued on the 7th, and in the second place, that as the sheriff was constantly on the move in pursuit, it must have been hard to catch him in the time which sufficed to send a message to a fixed point at Westminster.[1]

as it is in the present day. The relative price, however, depended so much on the commodities purchased that I hesitate to express myself positively on the subject. The only thing that I am quite clear about is that Father Gerard's estimate is greatly exaggerated. It is true that he grounds his errors on a statement by Dr. Jessopp that 4,000 marks was equivalent to 30,000*l.*, but the very exaggeration of these figures should have led him to suspect some error, or, at least —as I have recently been informed by Dr. Jessopp was the fact— that his calculation was based on other grounds than the relative price of commodities.

[1] Father Greenway's statement, that while the rebels were in the field, messengers came post haste continually one after the other, from the capital, all bearing proclamations mentioning Percy by name (*Gerard*, p. 155) is disposed of by the fact that there were only three proclamations in which Percy's name was mentioned, dated the 5th, the 7th, and the 8th. Percy was killed on the morning

It is needless to argue that Catesby was not the informer. The evidence is of the slightest, depending on the alleged statement by a servant,[1] long ago dead when it was committed to paper, and even Father Gerard appears hardly to believe that the charge is tenable.

There remains the case of Tresham. Since the publication of Jardine's work Tresham has been fixed on as the author or contriver of the letter to Monteagle which, according to the constant assertion of the Government, gave the first intimation of the existence of the plot, and this view of the case was taken by many contemporaries. Tresham was the last of three wealthy men—the others being Digby and Rokewood—who were admitted to the plot because their money could be utilised in the preparations for a rising. He was a cousin of Catesby and the two Winters, and had taken part in the negotiations with Spain before the death of Elizabeth. During the weeks immediately preceding November 5 there had been much searching of heart amongst the plotters as to the destruction in which Catholic peers would be involved, and it is probable that hints were given to some of them that it would be well to be absent from Parliament on the morning fixed for the explosion. Amongst the peers connected with

of the 8th, and even the messenger who started on the 7th can hardly have known that the sheriff had gone to Holbeche, and consequently could not himself have reached that place while Percy was living.

[1] See p. 11.

one or other of the plotters was Lord Monteagle, who had married Tresham's sister.

That Tresham should have desired to warn his brother-in-law was the most likely thing in the world. We know that he was in London on October 25 or 26, because Thomas Winter received 100*l.* from him on one of those days at his chambers in Clerkenwell.[1] It was in the evening of the 26th that Monteagle arrived at his house at Hoxton though he had not been there for more than twelve months. As he was sitting down to supper one of his footmen brought him a letter. Monteagle on receiving it, took the extraordinary course of handing it to one of his gentlemen named Ward, and bade him read it aloud. The letter was anonymous, and ran as follows :—

"My Lord, out of the love I bear to some of your friends, I have a care of your preservation. Therefore I would advise you, as you tender your life, to devise some excuse to shift of your attendance at this Parliament ; for God and man hath concurred to punish the wickedness of this time. And think not slightly of this advertisement but retire yourself into your country, where you may expect the event in safety, for though there be no appearance of any stir, yet I say they shall receive a terrible blow this Parliament, and yet they shall not see who hurts them. This counsel is not to be contemned, because it may do you good, and can do you no harm, for the danger is past as soon as you have burnt this letter ; and I hope

[1] T. Winter's examination, November 25 (*G. P. B.* No. 116). Compare Tresham's declaration of November 13 (*ib.* No. 63).

God will give you the grace to make good use of it, to whose holy protection I commend you."

Monteagle took the letter to Salisbury, and if the protestations of the Government are to be trusted, this was the first that Salisbury or any one of his fellow councillors heard of the conspiracy. Father Gerard follows Jardine and others in thinking this to be improbable if not incredible.

It may at least be freely granted that it is hardly probable that Monteagle had not heard of the plot before. As Jardine puts it forcibly:—

"The circumstance of Lord Monteagle's unexpected visit to his house at Hoxton, without any other assignable reason, on the evening in question, looks like the arrangement of a convenient scene; and it is deserving of notice that the gentleman to whom his lordship gave the letter to read at his table was Thomas Ward, an intimate friend of several of the conspirators, and suspected to have been an accomplice in the treason. The open reading of such a letter before his household (which, unless it be supposed to be part of a counterplot, seems a very unnatural and imprudent course for Lord Monteagle to adopt) might be intended to secure evidence that the letter was the first intimation he had of the matter, and would have the effect of giving notice to Ward that the plot was discovered, in order that he might communicate the fact to the conspirators. In truth he did so on the very next morning; and if they had then taken the alarm, and instantly fled to Flanders (as it is natural to suppose they would have done) every part of Tresham's object would have been attained. This scheme was frustrated by the unexpected and extraordinary infatuation of the conspirators themselves, who, notwithstanding their knowledge of the letter, disbelieved the discovery of the plot from the absence of any search at the cellar, and, omitting to avail themselves of the means afforded for their flight, still lingered in London." [1]

It is unnecessary to add any word to this, so far as it affects the complicity of Tresham with Monteagle. I submit, however, that the stronger is the evidence that the letter was prearranged with Monteagle the more hopeless is the reasoning of those who, like Father Gerard, hold that it was prearranged with Salisbury. Salisbury's object, according to Father Gerard's hypothesis, was to gain credit by springing upon the King and the world a partly or totally imaginary plot. If he was to do this, he must have some evidence to bring which would convince the world that the affair was not a mere imposture; and yet it is to be imagined that he contrives a scheme which threatens to leave him in possession of an obscure letter, and the knowledge that every one of the plotters was safely beyond the sea. As a plan concocted by Monteagle and Tresham to stop the plot, and at the same time secure the escape of their guilty friends, the little comedy at Hoxton was admirably concocted. From the point of view of the Government its advantages are not obvious. Add to this that all Salisbury's alleged previous knowledge did not enable him to discover that a mine had been dug till Fawkes told him

[1] Jardine's *Gunpowder Plot*, p. 91.

as late as November 8, and that the Government for two or three days after Fawkes was taken were in the dark as to the whereabouts of the conspirators, and we find every reason to believe that the statement of the Government, that they only learnt the plot through the Monteagle letter, was absolutely true.

That the Government dealt tenderly with Tresham in not sending him to the Tower till the 12th, and allowing him the consolation of his wife's nursing when he fell ill, is only what was to have been expected if they had learnt from Monteagle the source of his information, whilst they surely would have kept his wife from all access to him if he had had reason to complain to her that he had been arrested in spite of his services to the Government. After his death, which took place in the Tower, there was no further consideration of him, and, on December 23, the Council ordered that his head should be cut off and preserved till further directions, but his body buried in the Tower.[1]

It is unnecessary to go deeply into the question of the discrepancy between the different accounts given by the Government of the manner in which the Monteagle letter was expounded. The probable truth is that Salisbury himself interpreted it correctly, and that his fellow-councillors came to the same conclusion as himself. It was, however, a matter of etiquette to hold that the King was as sharp-witted as Elizabeth had been beautiful till the day of her death, and as the

[1] *Add. MSS.* 11,402, fol. 109.

solution of the riddle was not difficult, some councillor—perhaps Salisbury himself—may very well have suggested that the paper should be submitted to his Majesty. When he had guessed it, it would be also a matter of etiquette to believe that by the direct inspiration of God his Majesty had solved a problem which no other mortal could penetrate. We are an incredulous race nowadays, and we no more believe in the Divine inspiration of James I. than in the loveliness of Elizabeth at the age of seventy; and we even find it difficult to understand Father Gerard's seriousness over the strain which the poor councillors had to put upon themselves in fitting the facts to the courtly theory.

Nor is there any reason to be surprised at the postponement by the Government of all action to the night of November 4. It gave them a better chance of coming upon the conspirators preparing for the action, and if their knowledge was, as I hold it was, confined to the Monteagle letter, they may well have thought it better not to frighten them into flight by making premature inquiries. No doubt there was a danger of gunpowder exploding and blowing up not only the empty House of Lords, but a good many innocent people as well; but there had been no explosion yet, and the powder was in the custody of men whose interest it was that there should be no explosion before the 5th. After all, neither the King nor Salisbury, nor indeed any of the other councillors, lived near enough to be hurt by any accident that might occur. Smith's wildly improbable view that the shock might have 'levelled and destroyed all London and Westminster like an earthquake,' [1] can hardly be taken seriously.

We now come to the alleged discrepancies between various accounts of Fawkes's seizure. Father Gerard compares three documents—(*a*) what he terms 'the account furnished by Salisbury for the information of the King of France, November 6, 1605,' (*b*) the letter sent on November 9 to Edmondes and other ambassadors,[2] and (*c*) the King's Book. On the first, I would remark that there is no evidence, I may add, no probability, that, as it stands, it was ever despatched to France at all. It is a draft written on the 6th, which was gradually moulded into the form in which it was, as we happen to know, despatched on the 9th to Edmondes and Cornwallis. If the despatches received by Parry had been preserved, I do not doubt but that we should find that he also received it in the same shape as the other ambassadors.

Having premised this remark as a caution against examining the document too narrowly, we may admit that the three statements differ about the date at which the Monteagle letter was received—(*a*) says it was some four or five days before the Parliament; (*b*) that it was eight days; (*c*) that it was ten days. The third and latest statement is accurate; but the mistakes of

[1] Smith's *Antiquities of Westminster*, p. 41. [2] See p. 31.

the others are of no importance, except to show that the draft was carelessly drawn up, probably by Munck, Salisbury's secretary, in whose handwriting it is; and that the mistake was corrected with an approach to accuracy three days later, and made quite right further on.

With respect to the more important point raised by Father Gerard that—while (*a*) does not mention Suffolk's search in the afternoon, (*b*) does not mention the presence of Fawkes at the time of the afternoon visit—it is quite true that the hurried draft does not mention Suffolk's visit; but it is not true that it in any way denies the fact that such a visit had taken place.

Father Gerard abbreviates the story of (*a*) as follows:—

> "It was accordingly determined, the night before, 'to make search about that place, and to appoint a watch in the Old Palace to observe what persons might resort thereunto.'
>
> "Sir T. Knyvet, being appointed to the charge thereof, *going by chance, about midnight, into the vault, by another door,*[1] *found Fawkes within.* Thereupon he caused some few faggots to be removed, and so discovered some of the barrels, '*merely, as it were, by God's direction, having no other cause but a general jealousy.*'"[2]

The italics are Father Gerard's own, and I think we are fairly entitled to complain, so far as the first phrase thus distinguished is concerned, because being

[1] On this, see p. 110. [2] *Gerard*, p. 126, note 1.

printed in this manner it looks like a quotation, though as a matter of fact is not so. This departure from established usage is the more unfortunate, as the one important word—'chance'—upon which Father Gerard's argument depends, is a misprint or a miswriting for the word 'change,' which is to be seen clearly written in the MS. The whole passage as it there stands runs as follows:—

"This advertisement being made known to his Majesty and the Lords, their Lordships found not good, coming as it did in that fashion, to give much credit to it, or to make any apprehension of it by public show, nor yet so to contemn it as to do nothing at all in it, but found convenient the night before under a pretext that some of his Majesty's wardrobe stuff was stolen and embezzled to make search about that place, and to appoint a watch in the old palace to observe what persons might resort thereabouts, and appointed the charge thereof to Sir Thomas Knyvet, who about midnight going by change into the vault by another door, found the fellow, as is said before,[1] whereupon suspicion being increased, he caused some few faggots to be removed, and so discovered some of the barrels of powder, merely, as it were, by God's direction, having no other cause but a general jealousy."[2]

If the word 'chance' had been found in the real letter, it could hardly be interpreted otherwise than to

[1] In an earlier part of the letter we are told of 'Johnson,' that 'on Tuesday at midnight, as he was busy to prepare his things for execution was apprehended in the place itself, with a false lantern, booted and spurred.'

[2] *S. P. France.*

imply a negative of the earlier visit said to have been followed by a resolve on the King's part to search farther. As the word stands, it may be accepted as evidence that an earlier visit had taken place. How could Knyvet go 'by change' into the vault by another door, unless he or someone else had gone in earlier by some other approach? It is, however, the positive evidence which may be adduced from this letter, which is most valuable. The letter is, as I said, a mere hurried draft, in all probability never sent to anyone. It is moreover quite inartistic in its harking back to the story of the arrest after giving fuller details. Surely such a letter is better calculated to reveal the truth than one subsequently drawn up upon fuller consideration. What is it then, that stares us in the face, if we accept this as a genuine result of the first impression made upon the writer —whether he were Munck or Salisbury himself? What else than that the Government had no other knowledge of the plot than that derived from the Monteagle letter, and that not only because the writer says that the discovery of the powder was 'merely as it were, by God's direction, having no other cause but a general jealousy,' but because the whole letter, and still more the amplified version which quickly followed, is redolent with uncertainty. Given that Suffolk's mission in the afternoon was what it was represented to be, it becomes quite intelligible why the writer of the draft should be inclined to leave it unnoticed. It was an investigation made by men who were afraid of being blown up, but almost as much afraid of being made fools of by searching for gunpowder which had no existence, upon the authority of a letter notoriously ambiguous.

"And so," wrote Salisbury, in the letter despatched to the ambassadors on the 9th,[1] "on Monday in the afternoon, accordingly the Lord Chamberlain, whose office is to see all places of assembly put in readiness when the King's person shall come, took his coach privately, and after he had seen all other places in the Parliament House, he took a slight occasion to peruse that vault, where, finding only piles of billets and faggots heaped up, which were things very ordinarily placed in that room, his Lordship fell inquiring only who ought[2] the same wood, observing the proportion to be somewhat more than the housekeepers were likely to lay in for their own use; and answer being made before the Lord Monteagle, who was there present with the Lord Chamberlain, that the wood belonged to Mr. Percy, his Lordship straightway conceived some suspicion in regard of his person; and the Lord Monteagle also took notice that there was great profession between Percy and him, from which some inference might be made that it was a warning from a friend, my Lord Chamberlain resolved absolutely to proceed in a search, though no other materials were visible, and being returned to court about five o'clock took me up with him to the King and told him that, although he was hard of belief that any such thing was thought of, yet in such a case as this whatsoever was not done to put all out of doubt, was as good as nothing, whereupon it was resolved by his Majesty that this matter should

[1] See p. 31. I give the extract in the form received by Edmondes, that printed in *Winwood*, ii. 170, received by Cornwallis, being slightly different.

[2] *i.e.* 'owned.'

be so carried as no man should be scandalised by it, nor any alarm taken for any such purpose."

Even if it be credible that Salisbury had invented all this, it is incredible that if he alone had been the depository of the secret, he should not have done something to put other officials on the right track, or have put into the foreground his own clear-sightedness in the matter.

The last question necessary to deal with relates to the unimportant point where Fawkes was when he was arrested.

"To say nothing," writes Father Gerard, "of the curious discrepancies as to the date of the warning, it is clearly impossible to determine the locality of Guy's arrest. The account officially published in the 'King's Book,' says that this took place in the street. The letter to the ambassadors assigns it to the cellar and afterwards to the street; that to Parry to the cellar only. Fawkes himself, in his confession of November 5, says that he was apprehended neither in the street nor in the cellar, but in his own room in the adjoining house Chamberlain writes to Carleton, November 7, that it was in the cellar. Howes, in his continuation of Stowes' *Annals*, describes two arrests of Fawkes, one in the street, the other in his own chamber. This point, though seemingly somewhat trivial, has been invested with much importance. According to a time-honoured story, the baffled desperado roundly declared that had he been within reach of the powder when his captors appeared, he would have applied a match and involved them in his own destruction." [1]

This passage deserves to be studied, if only as a

[1] *Gerard*, p. 127.

good example of the way in which historical investigation ought not to be conducted, that is to say, by reading into the evidence what, according to preconception of the inquirer, he thinks ought to be there, but is not there at all. In plain language, the words 'cellar' and 'street' are not mentioned in any one of the documents cited by Father Gerard. There is no doubt a discrepancy, but it is not one between these two localities. The statements quoted by Father Gerard in favour of a capture in the 'cellar' merely say that it was effected 'in the place.' The letter of the 9th says 'in the place itself,'[1] and this is copied from the draft of the 6th. Chamberlain says[2] that Fawkes was 'taken making his trains at midnight,' but does not say where. Is it necessary to interpret this as meaning the 'cellar'? There was, as we know, a door out of the 'cellar' into the passage, and probably a door opposite into Percy's house. If Fawkes were arrested in this passage as he was coming out of the cellar and going into the house, or even if he had come out of the passage into the head of the court, he might very well be said to have been arrested 'in the place itself,' in contradistinction to a place a few streets off.

The only real difficulty is how to reconcile this account of the arrest, with Fawkes's own statement on his first examination on November 5, when he said:—

"That he meant to have fired the same by a match, and

[1] *Winwood*, ii. 170.
[2] Chamberlain to Carleton, November 7.—*S. P. Dom.* xvi. 23.

saith that he had touchwood and a match also, about eight or nine inches long, about him, and when they came to apprehend him he threw the touchwood and match out of the window in his chamber near the Parliament House towards the waterside."

Fawkes, indeed, was not truthful in his early examinations, but he had no inducement to invent this story, and it may be noted that whenever the accounts which have reached us go into details invariably they speak of two separate actions connected with the arrest. The draft to Parry, indeed, only speaks of the first apprehension, but the draft of the narrative which finally appeared in the King's Book [1] says that Knyvet 'finding the same party with whom the Lord Chamberlain before and the Lord Monteagle had spoken newly, come out of the vault, made stay of him.' Then Knyvet goes into the vault and discovers the powder. "Whereupon the caitiff being surely seized, made no difficulty to confess, &c." [2] The letter to the ambassadors [3] tells the same story. Knyvet going into the vault 'found that fellow Johnson newly come out of the vault, and without asking any more questions stayed him.' Then after the search 'he perceived the barrels and so bound the caitiff fast.' The King's Book itself separates at least the 'apprehending' from the searching.

"But before his entry into the house finding Thomas Percy's alleged man standing without the doors,[4] his

[1] See p. 99. [2] *G.P.B.* No. 129. [3] *Winwood* ii. 170.

[4] These words look as if he had been found not in the passage but in the court.

clothes and boots on at so dead a time of the night, he resolved to apprehend him, as he did, and thereafter went forward to the searching of the house . . . and thereafter, searching the fellow whom he had taken, found three matches, and all other instruments fit for blowing up the powder ready upon him."

All these are cast more or less in the same mould. On the other hand, a story, in all probability emanating from Knyvet, which Howes interpolated in a narrative based on the official account, gives a possibility of reconciling the usual account of the arrest with the one told by Fawkes. After telling, after the fashion of the King's Book, of Fawkes' apprehension and Knyvet's search, he bursts on a sudden into a narrative of which no official document gives the slightest hint:—

"And upon the hearing of some noise Sir T. Knyvet required Master Edmond Doubleday, Esq.[1] to go up into the chamber to understand the cause thereof, the which he did, and had there some speech of Fawkes, being therewithal very desirous to search and see what books or instruments Fawkes had about him; but Fawkes being wondrous unwilling to be searched, very violently griped M[aster] Doubleday by his fingers of the left hand, through pain thereof Ma[ster] Doubleday offered to draw his dagger to have stabbed Fawkes, but suddenly better bethought himself and did not; yet in that heat he struck up the traitor's heels and therewithal fell upon him and searched him, and in his pocket found his garters, wherewith

[1] He was a favourite dependent of Knyvet's, who, on April 10, 1604, had recommended him for an office in the Tower.—*S. P. Dom.* vii. 18.

M[aster] Doubleday and others that assisted they bound him. There was also found in his pocket a piece of touchwood, and a tinder box to light the touchwood and a watch which Percy and Fawkes had bought the day before, to try conclusions for the long or short burning of the touchwood, which he had prepared to give fire to the train of powder."

Surely this life-like presentation of the scene comes from no other than Doubleday himself, as he is the hero of the little scene. Knyvet plainly had not bound Fawkes when he 'stayed' or 'apprehended' him. He must have given him in charge of some of his men, who for greater safety's sake took him out of the passage or the court—whichever it was—into his own chamber within the house. Then a noise is heard, and Knyvet, having not yet concluded the examination, sends Doubleday to find out what is happening, with the result we have seen. When Knyvet arrives on the scene, he has Fawkes more securely bound than with a pair of garters. The only discrepancy remaining is between Fawkes's statement that he threw touchwood and match out of window, and Doubleday's that the touchwood at least was found in his pocket. Perhaps Doubleday meant only that the touchwood thrown out came from Fawkes's pocket. Perhaps there is some other explanation. After all, this is too trivial a matter to trouble ourselves about.

Wearisome as these details are, they at least bring once more into relief the hesitancy which characterises every action of the Government till the powder is actually discovered. Though Fawkes has been seen by Suffolk in the afternoon, no preparations are made for his arrest. Knyvet does not even bring cord with him to tie the wrists of a possible conspirator, and when Doubleday at last proceeds to bind him, he has to rely upon the garters found in his pocket. It is but one out of many indications which point to the conclusion that the members of the Government had nothing to guide their steps but an uncertain light in which they put little confidence. Taken together with the revelations of their ignorance as to the whereabouts of the plotters after Fawkes's capture had been effected, it almost irresistibly proves that they had no better information to rest on than the obscure communication which had been handed to Monteagle at Hoxton. As I have said before, the truth of the ordinary account of the plot would not be in the slightest degree affected if Salisbury had known of it six weeks or six months earlier. I feel certain, however, that he had no such previous knowledge, because, if he had, he would have impressed on the action of his colleagues the greater energy which springs from certainty. It is strange, no doubt, that a Government with so many spies and intelligencers afoot, should not have been aware of what was passing in the Old Palace of Westminster. It was, however, not the first or the last time that governments, keeping a watchful eye on the ends of the earth, have been in complete ignorance of what was passing under their noses.

CHAPTER VI

THE GOVERNMENT AND THE CATHOLICS

Having thus disposed of Father Gerard's assaults on the general truth of the accepted narrative of the Plot, we can raise ourselves into a larger air, and trace the causes leading or driving the Government into measures which persuaded such brave and constant natures to see an act of righteous vengeance in what has seemed to their own and subsequent ages, a deed of atrocious villainy. Is it true, we may fairly ask, that these measures were such as no honourable man could in that age have adopted, and which it is therefore necessary to trace to the vilest of all origins—the desire of a half-successful statesman to root himself in place and power ?

It would, indeed, be difficult to deny that the feeling of advanced English Protestants towards the Papal Church was one of doctrinal and moral estrangement. They held that the teaching of that church was false and even idolatrous, and they were quite ready to use the power of the state to extirpate a falsity so pernicious. On the other hand, the priests, Jesuits, and others, who flocked to England with their lives in their hands, were filled with the joy of those whose work it is to disseminate eternal truths, and to rescue souls, lost in heresy, from spiritual destruction.

The statesman, whether in his own person aggressively Protestant or not, was forced to consider this antagonism from a different point of view. The outbreak against Rome which had marked the sixteenth century had only partially a doctrinal significance. It meant also the desire of the laity to lower the authority of the clergy. Before the Reformation the clergy owed a great part of their power to the organisation which centred in Rome, and the only way to weaken that organisation, was to strengthen the national organisation which centred in the crown. Hence those notions of the Divine Right of Kings and of *Cujus regio ejus religio*, which, however theoretically indefensible, marked a stage of progress in the world's career. The question whether, in the days of Elizabeth, England should accept the authority of the Pope or the authority of the Queen, was political as much as religious, and it is no wonder that Roman Catholics when they burnt Protestants, they placed the religious aspect of the quarrel in the foreground; nor that Protestants when they hanged and disembowelled Roman Catholics, placed the political aspect in the foreground. As a matter of fact, these were but two sides of the shield. Protestants who returned to the Papal Church not merely signified the acceptance of certain doctrines which they had formerly renounced, but also accepted a different view of the relations between Church and State, and denied the sufficiency of the national Government to decide finally on all causes, ecclesiastical and civil, without appeal. If the religious teaching of the Reformed Church fell, a whole system of earthly government would fall with it.

To the Elizabethan statesman therefore the missionary priests who flocked over from the continent constituted the gravest danger for the State as well as for the Church. He was not at the bottom of his heart a persecutor. Neither Elizabeth nor her chief advisers, though, even in the early part of the reign, inflicting sharp penalties for the denial of the royal supremacy, would willingly have put men to death because they held the doctrine of transubstantiation, or any other doctrine which had found favour with the Council of Trent; but after 1570 they could not forget that Pius V. had excommunicated the Queen, and had, as far as his words could reach, released her subjects from the bond of obedience. Hence those excuses that, in enforcing the Recusancy laws against the Catholic laity, and, in putting Catholic priests to death as traitors, Elizabeth and her ministers were actuated by purely political motives. It was not exactly the whole truth, but there was a good deal more of truth in it than Roman Catholic writers are inclined to admit.

It was in this school of statesmanship that Sir Robert Cecil—as he was in Elizabeth's reign—had been brought up, and it was hardly likely that he would be willing to act otherwise than his father had done. It was, indeed, hard to see how the quarrel was to be lifted out of the groove into which it had sunk. How could statesmen be assured that, if the priests and Jesuits were allowed to extend their religious influence freely, the result would not be the destruction of the existing political system? That Cecil would have solved the problem is in any case most unlikely. It was, perhaps, too difficult to be as yet solved by any one, and Cecil was no man of genius to lead his age. Yet there were two things which made for improvement. In the first place, the English Government was immensely stronger at Elizabeth's death than it had been at her accession, and those who sat at the helm could therefore regard, with some amount of equanimity, dangers that had appalled their predecessors forty-five years before. The other cause for hope lay in the accession of a new sovereign; James had never been the subject of Papal excommunication as Elizabeth had been, and was consequently not personally committed to extreme views.

James's character and actions lend themselves so easily to the caricaturist, and so much that he did was the result either of egotistic vanity or of a culpable reluctance to take trouble, that it is difficult to give him credit for the good qualities that he really possessed. Yet hazy as his opinions in many respects were, it is easy to trace through his whole career a tolerably consistent principle. He would have been pleased to put an end, not indeed to the religious dispute, but to the political antagonism between those who were divided in religion, and would gladly have laid aside the weapon of persecution for that of argument. The two chief actions of his reign in England were the attempt to secure religious peace for his own dominions by an understanding with the Pope, and the attempt to secure a cessation of religious wars in Europe by an understanding with the King of Spain. In both cases is revealed a desire to obtain the co-operation of the leader of the party opposed to himself. Of course it is possible, perhaps even right, to say that this line of action was hopeless from the beginning, as involving too sanguine an estimate of the conciliatory feelings of those for whose co-operation he was looking. All that we are here concerned with is to point out that James brought with him ideas on the subject of the relations between an English—and, for the matter of that, a Scottish—king and the papacy, which were very different from those in which Cecil had been trained.

On the other hand, James's ideas, even when they had the element of greatness in them, never lifted him into greatness. He looked upon large principles in a small way, usually regarding them through the medium of his own interests. The doctrine that the national government ought to be supreme, took in his mind the shape of a belief that his personal government ought to be supreme. When in Scotland he sought an understanding with the

Pope, his own succession to the English Crown occupied the foreground, and the advantage of having the English Catholics on his side made him eager to strike a bargain. On the other hand, he refused to strike that bargain unless his own independent position were fully recognised. When, in 1599, he despatched Edward Drummond to Italy, he instructed him to do everything in his power to procure the elevation of a Scottish Bishop of Vaison to the Cardinalate, in order that he might advocate his interests at Rome. Yet he refused to write directly to the Pope himself, merely because he objected to address him as 'Holy Father.'[1] It was hardly the precise objection that would have been taken by a man of greater practical ability.

Nor was it only on niceties of this sort that James's desire to come to some sort of understanding with the Pope was likely to be wrecked. His correspondence with Cecil during the last years of Elizabeth, shows how little he had grasped the special difficulties of the situation, whilst on the other hand it throws light on the shades of difference between himself and his future minister. In a letter written to Cecil in the spring of 1602, James objects to the immediate conclusion of a peace with Spain on three grounds, the last being that the 'Jesuits, seminary priests, and that rabble, wherewith England is already too much infected, would then resort there in such swarms as the caterpillars or flies did in

[1] See my *History of England*, 1603–1642, i. 80, 81.

Egypt, no man any more abhorring them, since the Spanish practices was the greatest crime that ever they were attainted of, which now by this peace will utterly be forgotten.'

"And now," he proceeds, "since I am upon this subject, let the proofs ye have had of my loving confidence in you plead for an excuse to my plainness, if I freely show you that I greatly wonder from whence it can proceed that not only so great a flock of Jesuits and priests dare both resort and remain in England, but so proudly do use their functions through all the parts of England without any controlment or punishment these divers years past: it is true that for remedy thereof there is a proclamation lately set forth, but blame me not for longing to hear of the exemplary execution thereof, *ne sit lex mortua.* I know it may be justly thought that I have the like beam in my own eye, but alas, it is a far more barbarous and stiffnecked people that I rule over. St. George surely rides upon a towardly riding horse, where I am daily bursting in daunting a wild unruly colt, and I protest in God's presence the daily increase that I hear of popery in England, and the proud vauntery that the papists makes daily there of their power, their increase, and their combined faction, that none shall enter to be King there but by their permission; this their bragging, I say, is the cause that moves me, in the zeal of my religion, and in that natural love I owe to England, to break forth in this digression, and to forewarn you of these apparent evils."

To this Cecil replied as follows:—

"For the matter of priests, I will also clearly deliver your Majesty my mind. I condemn their doctrine, I detest their conversation, and I foresee the peril which the exercise of their function may bring to this island, only I confess that I shrink to see them die by dozens, when (at the last gasp) they come so near loyalty, only because I remember that mine own voice, amongst others, to the law (for their death) in Parliament, was led by no other principle than that they were absolute seducers of the people from temporal obedience, and consequent persuaders to rebellion, and which is more, because that law had a retrospective to all priests made twenty years before. But contrary-wise for that generation of vipers (the Jesuits) who make no more ordinary merchandise of anything than of the blood and crowns of princes, I am so far from any compassion, as I rather look to receive commandment from you to abstain than prosecute."

This plain language drove James to reconsider his position.

"The fear," he replied, "I have to be mistaken by you in that part of my last letter wherein I discover the desire I have to see the last edict against Jesuits and priests put in execution; the fear, I say, of your misconstruing my meaning hereon (as appears by your answer), enforceth me in the very throng of my greatest affairs to pen by post an answer and clear resolution of my intention. I did ever hate alike both extremities in any case, only allowing the midst for virtue, as by my book now lately published doth plainly appear. The like course do I hold in this particular. I will never allow in my conscience that the blood of any man shall be shed for diversity of opinions in religion, but I would be sorry that Catholics should so multiply as they might be able to practise their old principles upon us. I will never agree that any should die for error in faith against the first table, but I think they should not be permitted to commit works of rebellion against the second table. I would be sorry by the sword to diminish their number, but I would also be loth that, by so great connivance and oversight given unto them, their numbers should so increase in that land as by continual multiplication they might at least become masters, having already such a settled monarchy amongst them, as their archpriest with his twelve apostles keeping their terms in London, and judging all questions as well civil as spiritual amongst all Catholics. It is for preventing of their multiplying, and new set up empire, that I long to see the execution of the last edict against them, not that thereby I wish to have their heads divided from their bodies, but that I would be glad to have both their heads and bodies separated from this whole island and safely transported beyond seas, where they may freely glut themselves upon their imaginated gods. No! I am so far from any intention of persecution, as I protest to God I reverence their Church as our Mother Church, although clogged with many infirmities and corruptions, besides that I did ever hold persecution as one of the infallible notes of a false church. I only wish that such order might be taken as the land might be purged of such great flocks of them that daily diverts the souls of many from the sincerity of the Gospel, and withal, that some means might be found for debarring their entry again, at least in so great swarms. And as for the distinction of their ranks, I mean between the Jesuits and the secular priests, although I deny not that the Jesuits, like venomed wasps and firebrands of sedition, are far more intolerable than the other sort that seem to profess loyalty, yet is their so plausible profession the more to be distrusted that like married women or minors, whose vows are ever subject to the controlment of their husbands and tutors,[1]

[1] *I.e.* Guardians.

their consciences must ever be commanded and overruled by their Romish god as it pleases him to allow or revoke their conclusions."[1]

The agreement and disagreement between the two writers is easily traced in these words. Both are averse to persecute for religion. Both are afraid lest the extension of the firmly organised Roman Church should be dangerous to the State as well as to religion. On the other hand, whilst Cecil is content to plod on in the old ways, James vaguely adumbrates some scheme by which the priests, being banished, might be kept from returning, and thus the chance of a dangerous growth of their religion being averted, it would be possible to protect the existing forms of government without having recourse to the old persecuting laws. We feel, in reading James's words, that we are reading the phrases of a pedant who has not imagination enough to see how his scheme would work out in real life; but at all events we have before us, as we so often have in James's writings, a glimpse of new possibilities, and a desire to escape from old entanglements.

With such ideas floating in his mind, and with a strong desire to gain the support of the English Catholics to his succession, James may easily have given assurances to Thomas Percy of an intention to extend toleration to the English Catholics, which may have overrun his own somewhat fluid intentions, and

[1] *Correspondence of King James VI. with Sir Robert Cecil*, pp. 31 33, 36.

may very well have been interpreted as meaning more than his words literally meant. James's engagement to Percy's master, Northumberland, was certainly not devoid of ambiguity. "As for the Catholics," he wrote, "I will neither persecute any that will be quiet and give but an outward obedience to the law, neither will I spare to advance any of them that will by good service worthily deserve it."[1]

When James reached England in 1603 he seemed inclined to carry out his intentions. He is reported, at least, to have told Cecil in June that the fines were not to be levied, adding that he did not wish to make merchandise of consciences, nor to set a price on faith. Yet, in spite of this, the meshes of the administrative system closed him in, and the fines continued to be collected.[2] The result was the conspiracy of Copley and others, including Watson, a secular priest. This foolish plot was, however, betrayed to the Government by some of the Roman Catholic clergy, who were wise enough to see that any violence attempted against James would only serve to aggravate their lot.

The discovery that there were those amongst the priests who were ready to oppose disloyalty quickened James to carry out his earlier intention. On June 17 he informed Rosny, the French ambassador, of his intention to remit the recusancy fines, and, after some hesitation, he resolved to put his engagement in

[1] *Correspondence of King James VI. with Sir Robert Cecil*, p. 75.

[2] Degli Effetti to Del Bufalo, June $\frac{16}{26}$.—*Roman Transcripts, R.O.*

execution. On July 17, 1603, he allowed a deputation from the leading Catholics to be heard by the Privy Council in his own presence, and assured them that as long as they remained loyal subjects their fines would be remitted. If they would obey the law—in other words, if they would soil their consciences by attending church—the highest offices in the State should be open to them.[1] The assurance thus given was at once carried out as far as possible. The 20*l.* fines ceased, and the greater part of the two-thirds of the rents of convicted recusants were no longer required. If some of the latter were still paid, it is probable that this was only done in cases in which the rents had been granted to lessees on a fixed payment to the Crown by contracts which could not be broken.

Obviously there were two ways in which attempts might be made to obviate danger from Catholic disloyalty. Individual Catholics might be won over to confidence in the Government by the redress of personal grievances, or the Pope, as the head of the Catholic organisation, might be induced to prohibit conspiracies as likely to injure rather than to advance the cause which he had at heart. It is unnecessary to say that the latter was a more delicate operation than the former.

An opening, indeed, had been already given. When James refused to sign a letter to Pope Clement VIII., on the ground that he could not address him as 'Holy

[1] Degli Effetti to Del Bufalo, July $\frac{21}{31}$.—*Roman Transcripts, R.O.*

Father,"[1] his secretary, Elphinstone, surreptitiously procured his signature, and sent it off without his knowledge.[2] Clement, therefore, was under the impression that he had received a genuine overture from James, and replied by a complimentary letter, which he intrusted to Sir James Lindsay, a Scottish Catholic then in Rome. In 1602 Lindsay reached Scotland, and delivered his letter. As he was to return to Rome, James instructed him to ask Clement to excuse him for not writing in reply, and for being unable to accept some proposal contained in the Pope's letters, the reasons in both cases having been verbally communicated to Lindsay. Finally, Lindsay was to assure Clement that James was resolved to observe two obligations inviolably. In the first place he would openly and without hypocrisy declare his opinion, especially in such matters as bore upon religion and conscience. In the second place, that his opinion might not be too obstinate where reason declared against it, he would, laying aside all prejudice, admit whatever could be clearly proved by the laws and reason.[3]

It is no wonder that James had rejected the Pope's proposal, as Clement had not only offered to oppose all James's competitors for the English succession, but had declared his readiness to send him money on condition that he would give up his eldest son to be educated as

[1] See p. 142. [2] *Hist. of England*, 1603-1642, i. 81.
[3] S. P. Scotland, lxix. 20.

Clement might direct.[1] That such a proposal should have been made ought to have warned James that it was hopeless to attempt to come to an understanding with the Pope on terms satisfactory to a Protestant Government. For a time no more was heard of the matter. Lindsay was taken ill, and was unable to start before James was firmly placed on the English throne.

The announcement to the lay Catholics that their fines would be remitted had been preluded by invitations to James to come to terms with the authorities of the Papal Church. Del Bufalo, Bishop of Camerino, the Nuncio at Paris, despatched a certain Degl' Effetti to England in Rosny's train, to feel the way, and the Nuncio at Brussels sent over his secretary, Sandrino, to inquire, though apparently without the sanction of the Pope himself, whether James would be willing to receive a '*legate*,'[2] which may probably be interpreted merely as a negotiator, not as a 'legate' in the full sense of the term. On July $\frac{11}{21}$, Del Bufalo, writing to Cardinal Aldobrandino, reports that the strongest argument used by James against toleration for the Catholics was, that if they were allowed to live in Catholic fashion

[1] James I. to Sir T. Parry, Nov., 1603.—Tierney's *Dodd*, iv.; App. p. 66.

[2] Degli Effetti to Del Bufalo, $\frac{\text{June 30,}}{\text{July 10.}}$ (*Roman Transcripts, R.O.*). There is a plain-spoken marginal note in the Pope's hand, 'Non sarà vero, nè noi gli habbiamo dato quest' ordine.' In the instructions by the Nuncio at Brussels to Dr. Gifford, $\frac{\text{July 22,}}{\text{August 1.}}$ (Tierney's *Dodd*, iv.; App. lxvi.), nothing is said about this mission, but a definite promise is given 'eosque omnes e regno evocare quos sua Majestas rationabiliter judicaverit regno et statui suo n xios fore.'

they must obey the Pope, and consequently disobey the King; whilst those who were favourable to toleration were of opinion that this argument would be deprived of strength if James could be assured that the Pope might remove this impediment by commanding Catholics under the highest possible penalty, to make oath of fidelity and obedience to his Majesty. When this reached Rome the following note was written on it in the Pope's hand :—

> "It is rather heresy which leads to disobedience. The Catholic religion teaches obedience to Princes, and defends them. As to reaching the King's ears, we shall be glad to do so, and we wish him to know with what longing for the safety[1] and quiet of himself and his kingdom we have proceeded and are proceeding. It is our conscientious desire so to proceed as we have written to one king and the other."[2]

As the letter referred to must have been the one in which Clement asked to have the education of Prince Henry, this note does not sound very promising. Nor was James's language, on the other hand, such as would be counted satisfactory at Rome. After his return from England Rosny informed Del Bufalo that James had assured him that he would not persecute the Catholics as long as they did not trouble the realm, and had praised the Pope as a temporal sovereign, adding

[1] 'Salute.' Does this mean safety or salvation, or is it left doubtful?

[2] *I.e.* to James and to Henry IV. Del Bufalo to Cardinal Aldobrandino, July $\frac{11}{21}$.—*Roman Transcripts, R.O.*

that if he could find a way of agreeing with him he would gladly adopt it, provided that he might remain at the head of his own Church.[1]

A letter written on August $\frac{8}{18}$, by Barneby, a priest recently liberated from prison, to Del Bufalo, throws further light on the situation. From this it appears that what the Nuncio at Brussels had proposed was not the sending of a fully authorised legate to England, but merely the appointment of someone who, being a layman, would, without offending James's susceptibility, be at hand to plead the cause of the Catholics and to give account of anything relating to their interests. We are thus able to understand how it was that the Nuncio had made the proposal without special orders from the Pope. More germane to the present inquiry is the account given by Barneby of James's own position:—

"For though," he writes, "it is certain that his Majesty conscientiously follows a religion contrary to us, and will therefore, as he says, never suffer his subjects to exercise lawfully and freely any other religion than his own—and that, both on account of his civil position, as on account of certain reasons and considerations relating to his conscience—nevertheless he openly promises to persecute no one on the ground of religion. And this he has so far happily begun to carry out with great honour to himself, and with the greatest joy advantage and pleasure to ourselves, though some of our most truculent enemies revolt, desiring that nothing but fine and sword may be

[1] Del Bufalo to Cardinal Aldobrandino, July $\frac{20}{30}$.—*Roman Transcripts, R.O.*

used against us. What will happen in the end I can hardly imagine before the meeting of Parliament.[1] "

As far as it is possible to disengage James's real intentions from these words, it would seem that he had positively declared against liberty of worship, but that he would not levy the legal fines for not going to church on those who remained obedient subjects. Did he mean to wink at the Mass being said in the private houses of the recusants, or at the activity of the priests in making converts? These were the questions he would have to face before he was out of his difficulties.

On the other side of the channel Del Bufalo was doing his best to convey assurances to James of the Pope's desire to keep the English Catholics in obedience. With this view he communicated with James's ambassador in Paris, Sir Thomas Parry, who on August 20, gave an account of the matter to Cecil:—

"The Pope's Nuncio," he wrote, "sent me a message, the effect whereof was that he had received authority and a mandate from Rome to call out of the King our master's dominions the factious and turbulent priests and Jesuits, and that, at M. de Rosny's[2] passage into the realm, he had advertised them thereof by a gentleman of his train, and that he was desirous to continue that service to the King, and further to stop such as at Rome shall move any suit with any such intent, and would advertise his Majesty of it; that he had stayed two English monks in that city whose names he sent me in writing, who had procured hereto-

[1] Barneby to Del Bufalo, Aug. $\frac{8}{18}$.—*Roman Transcripts*, *R.O.* (The original is in Latin.)

[2] Afterwards Duke of Sully.

fore faculty from thence to negotiate in England among the Catholics for such bad purposes; that not long since a petition had been exhibited to the Pope for assistance of the English Catholics with money promising to effect great matters for advancement of the Catholic cause upon receipt thereof; that his Holiness had rejected the petition and sharply rebuked the movers; that he would no more allow those turbulent courses to trouble the politic governments of Christian Princes, but by charitable ways of conference and exhortation seek to reduce them to unity. Lastly his request was to have this message related to the King, offering for the first trial of his sincere meaning that, if there remained any in his dominions, priest or Jesuit, or other busy Catholic, whom he had intelligence of for a practice in the state which could not be found out, upon advertisement of the names he would find means that by ecclesiastical censures they should be delivered unto his justice." [1]

The last words are somewhat vague, and as we have not the Nuncio's own words, but merely Parry's report of them, we cannot be absolutely certain what were the exact terms offered, or how far they went beyond the offers previously made by the Nuncio at Brussels.[2] Nor does a letter written by the Nuncio to the King on Sept. $\frac{19}{29}$, throw any light on the subject, as Del Bufalo confines himself to general expressions of the duty of Catholics to obey the King.[3] That the

[1] Parry to Cecil, Aug. 20, 1603.—*S. P. France.*

[2] See p. 151, note 2.

[3] Del Bufalo to James I. Sept. $\frac{19}{19}$; *compare* Del Bufalo to Cardinal Aldobrandino, $\frac{\text{Sept. 21}}{\text{Oct. 1}}$.—*Roman Transcripts*, *R.O.*

Nuncio's proposals met with considerable resistance among James's councillors is not only probable in itself, but is shown by the length of time which intervened before an answer was despatched at the end of November or the beginning of December.[1] The covered language with which Cecil opened the despatch in which he forwarded to Parry the letter giving the King's authorisation to the ambassador to treat with the Nuncio, leaves no doubt as to his own feelings.

> "But now, Sir," writes Cecil, "I am to deliver you his Majesty's pleasure concerning a matter of more importance, though for mine own part it is so tender as I could have wished I had little dealt in it ; not that the King doth not most prudently manage it, as you see, but because envious men suspect verity itself."

Parry, Cecil went on to say, was to offer to the Nuncio a Latin translation of the King's letter, and also to give him a copy of the instructions formerly given to Sir James Lindsay. The object of this was to prevent Lindsay from going beyond them. Cecil then proceeds to hint that Lindsay, who was now at last about to start from Italy, would not have been allowed to meddle further in the business but that it would disgrace him if he were deprived of the

[1] We have two copies of James's letter to Parry translated into Latin, but undated (*S. P. France.*) Cecil's covering letter (*ib.*) is in draft and dated Nov. 6. It must, however, have been held back, as both Parry's and Del Bufalo's despatches show that it did not reach Paris till early in December.

mission with which he had formerly been intrusted. The main negotiation, however, was to pass between Parry and the Nuncio, though only by means of a third person; and, as a matter of fact, Lindsay did not start for many months to come.

So far as concerns us, the King's letter accepts the Pope's objections to the sending of a 'legatus,' as he would be unable to show him proper respect; and then proceeds to contrast the Catholics who are animated by pure religious zeal with those who have revolutionary designs. With respect to both of these he professes his readiness to deal in such a way that neither the Pope nor any right minded or sane man shall be able to take objection. In an earlier part of the letter he had assumed that the Pope was prepared actually to excommunicate those Catholics who were of an unquiet and turbulent disposition. Whether this were justified or not by the Nuncio's words, it was an exceedingly large assumption that the Pope would bind himself to excommunicate Catholics practically at the bidding of a Protestant king.

On or about December $\frac{4}{14}$, 1604, the King's letter was forwarded by the Nuncio to Rome.[1] Nor did James confine his assurances to mere words. A person who left England on January 11,[2] 1604, assured the Nuncio that peaceful Catholics were living quietly, and that those who were devout were able 'to serve God accord-

[1] Del Bufalo to Cardinal Aldobrandino, December $\frac{4}{14}$.—*Roman Transcripts, R.O.*

[2] January $\frac{11}{21}$.

ing to their consciences without any danger.' He himself, he added, could bear witness to this, as, during the whole time he had been in London, he had heard mass daily in the house of one Catholic or another.[1]

This idyllic state of things — from the Roman Catholic point of view—was soon to come to an end. Clement VIII. refused, at least for the present, either to send a representative to England or to promise to call off turbulent persons under pain of excommunication.[2] Possibly nothing else was to be expected, as the idea of turning the Pope into a kind of spiritual policeman was not a happy one. Still, it is easy to understand that James must have felt mortified at the Pope's failure to respond to his overtures, and it is easy, also, to understand that Cecil would take advantage of the King's irritation for furthering his own aims. Nor were other influences wanting to move James in the same direction. Sir Anthony Standen had lately returned from a mission to Italy, and had brought with him certain relics as a present to the Queen, who was a Roman Catholic, and had entered into communication with Father Persons. Still more disquieting was

[1] Information given to Del Bufalo.

[2] He wrote on the margin of Del Bufalo's letter: "Quanto alla facoltà di chiamare sotto pena di scomunica i torbolenti, non ci par da darla per adesso, perchè trattiamo con heretici, e corriamo pericolo di perdere i sicuri, si come non ci par che il Nuntio debba premere nella cosa di mandar noi personaggio, perchè dubitiamo che essendo tanta gelosia tra Francia e Spagna non intrassimo in grandissima difficoltà. E meglio aspettare la conclusione dell a Pace secondo noi, perchè non sapiamo che chi mandassimo fosse per usar la prudentia necessaria."

it that a census of recusants showed that their numbers had very considerably increased since the King's accession. No doubt many of those who apparently figured as new converts were merely persons who had concealed their religion as long as it was unsafe to avow it, and who made open profession of it when no unpleasant consequences were to be expected; but there can also be little doubt that the number of genuine conversions had been very large. From the Roman Catholic point of view, this was a happy result of a purely religious nature. From the point of view of an Elizabethan statesman, it constituted a grave political danger. It is unnecessary here to discuss the first principles of religious toleration. It is enough to say that no Pope had reprimanded Philip II. for refusing to allow the spread of Protestantism in his dominions, and that James's councillors, as well as James himself, might fairly come to the conclusion that if the Roman Catholics of England increased in future years as rapidly as they had increased in the first year of the reign, it would not be long before a Pope would be found ready to launch against James the excommunication which had been launched against Elizabeth, and that his throne would be shaken, together with that national independence which that throne implied.

For the time James—pushed hard by his councillors,[1]

[1] He told the Spanish Ambassador, 'che quelli del Consiglio gli havevano fatto tanta forza che no haveva potuto far altro, ma che no si sarebbe eseguito con rigore alcuno.' (Del Bufalo to Aldobrandino $\frac{\text{March 27}}{\text{April 6}}$.—*Roman Transcripts, R.O.*

as he was—might fancy that he had found a compromise. There was to be no enforcement of the recusancy laws against the laity, but on February 22, 1604, a proclamation was issued ordering the banishment of the priests.[1] It was not a compromise likely to be of long endurance. For our purposes the most important of its results was that it produced the Gunpowder Plot. A few days after its issue that meeting of the five conspirators took place behind St. Clement's, at which they received the sacrament in confirmation of their mutual promise of secrecy. All that has been said of the tyranny of the penal laws upon the laity, as affording a motive for the plot, is so much misplaced rhetoric. Moreover, if we accept Fawkes's evidence[2] of the date at which he first heard of the plot as being about Easter, 1604, *i.e.* about April 8, the communication of the design to Winter must have taken place towards the end of March, that is to say after the issue of the proclamation and before any other step had been taken to enforce the penal laws. Consequently all arguments, attributing the invention of the plot to Cecil for the sake of gaining greater influence with the King fall to the ground. He had just achieved a triumph of no common order, the prelude, as he must have been keen enough to discern, of greater triumphs to come. Granted, for argument's sake, that Cecil was

[1] Precisely the course he had recommended in his letter written to Cecil whilst he was still in Scotland, see p. 144.

[2] See p. 33.

capable of any wickedness—we at least require some motive for the crime which Father Gerard attributes to him by innuendo.

As time went on, there was even less cause for the powerful minister to invent or to foster a false plot. It is unnecessary to tell again in detail the story which I have told elsewhere of the way in which James fell back upon the Elizabethan position, and put in force once more the penal laws against the laity. On November 28, 1604, he decided on requiring the 20*l.* fines from the thirteen wealthy recusants who were liable to pay them, and on February 10, 1605 [1]—a few days after the plotters had got half through the wall of the House of Lords—he announced his resolution that the penal laws should be put in execution. On May 4, 1605, Cecil, who in August, 1604, had been made Viscount Cranborne, was raised to the Earldom of Salisbury. Yet this is the politician who is supposed by Father Gerard to have been necessitated to keep himself in favour by the atrocious wickedness he is pleased to ascribe to him. In plain truth, Salisbury did not need to gain favour and power. He had both already.

A policy of intolerance is so opposed to the instincts of the present day, that it is worth while to hear a per-

[1] A news-letter gives an account of the Council meeting, from which it appears that James began by haranguing against the Puritans, but Cranborne—Cecil was now known by this title—and others asked why the Catholics were not put on the same footing, on which the King got angry, and finally directed that the Catholics should also suffer. (Advices from London, $\frac{\text{Feb. 19}}{\text{March 1}}$).—*Roman Transcripts, R.O.*

secutor in his own defence. On March 7, 1605, less than a month after the King's pronouncement, Nicolo Molin, the Venetian ambassador, writes, that he had lately spoken to Cranborne on the recent treatment of the Catholics.

"He replied that, through the too great clemency of the King, the priests had gone with great freedom through all the country, the City of London and the houses of many citizens, to say mass, which they had done with great scandal, and thereupon had arrived advices from Rome that the Pope had constituted a congregation of Cardinals to treat of the affairs of this kingdom which gave occasion to many to believe that the King was about to grant liberty of conscience,[1] and had caused a great stir amongst our Bishops and other ministers, the Pope having come to this resolution mainly through the offices of that light-headed man Lindsay,[2] and then his Majesty, whose thoughts were far from it, resolved to use a rather unusual diligence to restrict a little the liberty of these priests of yours, as also to assure those of our religion that there was not the least thought of altering things in this direction. Sir James Lindsay, he said, had disgusted his Majesty, and the Pope would in the end discover that he was a light-headed, unstable man. I understood, said I, that he had gone to Rome with the King's permission. It is quite true, said he, and if your Lordship wishes to understand the matter I will explain it. Sir James Lindsay, he continued, a year before the death of Queen Elizabeth asked

[1] In those days liberty of conscience meant what we should call liberty of worship.

[2] Lindsay at last got off to Rome in November 1604. On his proceedings there see *History of England*, 1603–1642, i. 224.

leave to go to Rome, and his request was easily granted. When he arrived there he got means, with the help of friends, to be introduced to the Pope to whom, as is probable, he addressed many impertinencies, as he has done at the present time. In short, he was presented to the Pope, and got from him a good sum of money, perhaps promising to do here what he will never do, and obtained an autograph letter from the Pope to our King to the effect that he had understood from Sir James Lindsay his Majesty's good disposition, if not to favour the Catholic religion, at least not to persecute it, for which he felt himself to be under great obligations to him, and promised to assist him when Queen Elizabeth died, and to help him as far as possible to gain the succession to her realm as was just and reasonable, but that if his Majesty would consent to have the Prince, his son, educated in the Catholic religion, he would bind himself to engage his state and life to assist him, and would do what he could [1] that the Christian Princes should act in union with the same object.[2] With this letter Sir James arrived, two months before the Queen's death, repeating to his Majesty many things besides to the same effect. The King was willing enough to look at the letter, as coming from a Prince, and filled with many affectionate and courteous expressions, but he never thought of answering it, though he was frequently solicited by Sir James. The reason of this was that it would be necessary in writing to the Pope to give him his titles of Holiness and Blessedness, to which, being held by

[1] In the MS. 'et non haverebbe.' Mr. Rawdon Brown, amongst whose papers, now in the Record Office, this despatch is found, remarks that mistakes of this kind frequently occur in letters first ciphered and then deciphered.

[2] In the margin is 'Questo poi è troppo,' perhaps an addition by the ambassador, or even by Mr. Rawdon Brown.

us to be impertinent, after the teaching of our religion, his Majesty could not be in any way persuaded, so that the affair remained asleep till the present time. Then came the Queen's death, on which Sir James again urged the King to answer the letter, assuring him that he would promise himself much advantage from the Pope's assistance if occasion served ; but it pleased God to show such favour to the King that he met with no opposition, as every one knows. Some months ago, however, it again occurred to Sir James to think of going to Rome ; he asked licence from his Majesty, and obtained it courteously enough. At his departure he said, 'I shall have occasion to see the Pope, and am certain that he will ask me about that letter of his. What answer am I to make ?' 'You are to say, replied the King, 'that you gave me the letter, and that I am much obliged to him for the love and affection he has shown me, to which I shall always try to correspond effectually.' 'Sire,' said Sir James, 'the Pope will not believe me. Will your Majesty find some means of assuring the Pope of the truth of this ?' On which his Majesty took the pen and drew up a memoir with his own hand, telling Sir James that if he had occasion to talk to the Pope he should assure him of his desire to show, by acts, the good will of which he spoke, and the esteem he felt for him as a temporal Prince. He then directed Sir James to dwell on this as much as he could, and that as to religion[1] he wished to preserve and maintain that in which he had been brought up, being assured that it was the best, but that, not having a sanguinary disposition, he had not persecuted the Catholics in their property or their life, as long as they remained obedient subjects. As to instructing the Prince, his son, in the Catholic religion, he would never do it,

[1] 'Religione' is suggested by Mr. Rawdon Brown for the 'ragione' of the decipherer.

because he believed it would bring down on him a heavy punishment from God, and the reproach of the world, if he were willing, whilst he himself professed a religion as the best, to promise that his son should be brought up in one full of corruptions and superstitions. Cecil then recounted the substance of the memoir, which was sealed with the King's seal, in order that the Pope and every one else might give credence to it on these points. Now, Sir James, to gain favour and get money, has transgressed these orders, as we understand that he has given occasion to the Pope to appoint a congregation of Cardinals on our affairs, and to us to have our eyes a little more open to the Catholics, and especially to the priests. To this I replied that I did not think that his Majesty should for this reason act against his constant professions not to wish to take any one's property or life, on account of religion. 'Sir,' he replied, 'be content as to blood, so long as the Catholics remain quiet and obedient. As to property, it is impossible to do less than observe [1] the laws in this respect, but even in that we shall proceed dexterously and much more gently than in the times of the late Queen, as the Catholics who refuse to attend our churches, and who are rich, will not think it much to pay £20 a month. Those who are less rich and have not the means to pay as much, and from whom two thirds of their revenue is taken during their lifetime will now have this advantage by the King's clemency that whereas in the Queen's time their property was granted to strangers who, to get as much as they could, did not hesitate to ruin their houses and possessions, it will now be granted to their own patrons, at the lowest rate, so that they will pay rather a quarter than two thirds of their estate. This arrangement has been

[1] In the copy 'non si può far di meno di non observar le leggi,' the 'non' being incorrectly repeated.

come to in order not to afflict the Catholics too much, and to prevent our own people from believing that we wish to give liberty to the Catholic religion, as they undoubtedly will if the payments are absolutely abolished."

After a further remonstrance from the ambassador, Cranborne returned to the charge.

"Sir," he replied, "nothing else can be done. These are the laws, and they must be observed. Their object is undoubtedly to extinguish the Catholic religion in this kingdom, because we do not think it fit, in a well-governed monarchy, to increase the number of persons who profess to depend on the will of other Princes as the Catholics do, the priests not preaching anything more constantly than this, that the good Catholic ought to be firmly resolved in himself to be ready to rise for the preservation of his religion even against the life and state of his natural Prince.[1] This is a very perilous doctrine, and we will certainly never admit it here, but will rather do our best to overthrow it, and we will punish most severely those who teach it and impress it on the minds of good subjects.[1]

It is unnecessary to pursue the conversation further, or even to discuss how far Cranborne was serious when he expressed his intention of moderating the incidence of the laws which the Government had resolved to carry out. It is certain that they were not so moderated, and

[1] "Non predicando li preti nessuna cosa più constantemente di questa che il buon Cattolico bisogna che habbia questa ferma rissolutione in se medesimo di esser per conservar la Religione pronto a solevarsi etiam contra la vita e stato del suo Principe naturale."

[2] Molin to the Doge, March $\frac{7}{17}$, 1605, *Venetian Transcripts, R.O.*

that the enforcement of law rapidly degenerated into mere persecution. What is important for our purposes is that the language I have just quoted leads us to the bed-rock of the situation. Between Pope and king a question of sovereignty had arisen, a question which could not be neglected without detriment to the national independence till the Pope either openly or tacitly abandoned his claim to excommunicate kings, and to release such subjects as looked up to him for guidance from the duty of obedience to their King. That the Pope should openly abandon this claim was more than could be expected; but he had not excommunicated James as his predecessor had excommunicated Elizabeth, and there was some reason to hope that he might allow the claim to be buried in oblivion. At all events, Clement VIII. had not only refused to excommunicate James, but had enjoined on the English Catholics the duty of abstaining from any kind of resistance to him. James had, however, wished to go further. Incapable—as most people in all ages are—of seeing the position with other eyes than his own, he wanted the Pope actively to co-operate with him in securing the obedience of his subjects. He even asked him to excommunicate turbulent Catholics, a thing to which it was impossible for the Pope—who also looked on these matters from his own point of view—to consent. In the meanwhile it was becoming evident that the Pope was not working for a Protestant England under a Protestant king, with a Catholic minority accepting what crumbs of toleration that king might fling to them, and renouncing for ever the right to resist his laws however oppressive they might be; but rather for a Catholic England under a Catholic King. This appeared in Clement's demand that Prince Henry should be educated in a religion which was not that of his father, and it appeared again in the reports of Lindsay, which had caused such a commotion at Whitehall. "His Holiness," wrote Lindsay, "hath commanded to continue to pray for your Majesty, and he himself stays every night two large hours in prayer for your Majesty, the Queen, and your children, and for the conversion of your Majesty and your dominions. This I may very well witness as one who was present."[1] We should have thought the worse of the Pope if he had done otherwise; but the news of it was hardly likely to be welcome to an English statesman. Who was to guarantee that, if the priests were allowed full activity in England a Roman Catholic majority would not be secured—or, that when such a majority was secured, the suspended excommunication would not be launched, and a rebellion, such as that of the League in France, encouraged against an obstinately Protestant Sovereign. We may be of opinion that those statesmen who attempted to meet the danger with persecution were men of little faith, who might have trusted to the strength of their religious and political

[1] Lindsay to James I. $\frac{\text{Jan. 26}}{\text{Feb. 5}}$, 1605, *S. P. Italian States.*

creed—the two could not in those days be separated from one another; but there can be no doubt that the danger was there. We may hold Salisbury to have been but a commonplace man for meeting it as he did, but he had on his side nearly the whole of the official class which had stood by the throne of Elizabeth, and which now stood by the throne of James.

At all events, Salisbury's doctrine that there was to be no personal understanding with the Pope was the doctrine which prevailed then and in subsequent generations. James's attempt came to nothing through its insuperable difficulties, as well as through his own defects of character. A pleading, from a Roman Catholic point of view, in favour of such an understanding may be found in a letter written by Sir Everard Digby to Salisbury, which Father Gerard has shown to have been written, not in December, as Mrs. Everett Green suggested, but between May 4 and September, 1605, and which I ascribe to May, or as soon after May as is possible. The letter, after a reference to a conversation recently held between Digby himself and Salisbury, proceeds as follows:—

"One part of your Lordship's speech, as I remember, was that the King could not get so much from the Pope (even then, when his Majesty had done nothing against the Catholics) as a promise that he would not excommunicate him, wherefore it gave occasion to suspect that, if Catholics were suffered to increase, the Pope might afterwards proceed to excommunication if the King would not change his religion.[1] But to take away that doubt, I do assure myself that his Holiness may be drawn to manifest so contrary a disposition of excommunicating the King, that he will proceed with the same course against all as shall go about to disturb the King's quiet and happy reign[2]; and the willingness of Catholics, especially of priests and Jesuits, is such as I dare undertake to procure any priest in England (though it were the Superior of the Jesuits) to go himself to Rome to negotiate this business, and that both he and all other religious men (till the Pope's pleasure be known) shall take any spiritual course to stop the effect that may proceed from any discontented or despairing Catholic.

"And I doubt not but his return would bring both assurance that such course should not be taken with the King, and that it should be performed against any that should seek to disturb him for religion. If this were done, there could then be no cause to fear any Catholic, and this may be done only with those proceedings (which, as I understood your Lordship) should be used. If your Lordship apprehend it to be worth the doing I shall be glad to be the instrument, for no hope to put off from myself any punishment, but only that I wish safety to the King and ease to the Catholics. If your Lordship and the State think it fit to deal severely with Catholics within brief there will be massacres, rebellions and desperate attempts against the King and State. For it is a general received reason amongst Catholics that there is not that expecting and suffering course now to be run that was in the Queen's time, who was the last of her line, and the last in expectance to run violent courses against Catholics; for

[1] Compare the last passage quoted from Molin's despatch, p. 161.

[2] This is, however, precisely what James had failed to induce the Pope to do.

then it was hoped that the King that now is would have been at least free from persecuting, as his promise was before his coming into this realm, and as divers his promises have been since his coming, saying that he would take no soul-money nor blood. Also, as it appeared, was the whole body of the Council's pleasure when they sent for divers of the better sort of Catholics (as Sir Thomas Tresham and others) and told them it was the King's pleasure to forgive the payment of Catholics, so long as they should carry themselves dutifully and well. All these promises every man sees broken, and to thrust them further in despair, most Catholics take note of a vehement book written by Mr. Attorney, whose drift (as I have heard) is to prove that only being a Catholic is to be a traitor, whose book coming forth after the breach of so many promises, and before the ending of such a violent Parliament, can work no less effect in men's minds than a belief that every Catholic will be brought within that compass before the King and State have done with them. And I know, as the priest himself told me, that if he had not hindered, there had somewhat been attempted, before our offence,[1] to give ease to Catholics. But being so safely prevented, and so necessary to avoid, I doubt not but your Lordship and the rest of the Lords will think of a more mild and undoubted safe course, in which I will undertake the performance of what I have promised, and as much as can be expected; and when I have done I shall be as willing to die as I am ready to offer my service, and expect not nor desire favour for it, either before the doing

[1] Father Gerard asks what 'our offence' was. It was clearly nothing personal to the writer, and I am strongly inclined to interpret the words as referring to Lindsay's proceedings at Rome, of which so much had been made.

it, nor in the doing it, nor after it is done, but refer myself to the resolved course for me."[1]

I have thought it well to set forth the pleadings on both sides, though it has led me somewhat out of my appointed track. Though our sympathies are with the weaker and oppressed party, it cannot be said that Digby's letter meets the whole case which Salisbury had raised. Whether that be so or not, it is enough, for our present purpose if we are able to discern that Salisbury had a case, and was not merely manœuvring for place or power. At all events, his opinion, whether it were bad or good, had, in the spring of 1605, been accepted by James, and he was therefore in less need even than in the preceding year of producing an imaginary or half-imaginary plot to frighten to his side a king who had already come round to his ideas.

[1] Sir Everard Digby to Salisbury (*S. P. Dom.* xvii. 10.) As Father Gerard says, the date cannot be earlier than May 4, 1605, when the Earldom was conferred on Cranborne.

CHAPTER VII

THE GOVERNMENT AND THE PRIESTS

It was unavoidable that the persecution to which Catholics were subjected should bear most hardly on the priests, who were held guilty of disseminating a disloyal religion. It is therefore no matter for surprise that we find, about April 1604,[1] an informer, named Henry Wright, telling Cecil that another informer named Davies, was able to set, *i.e.* to give information of the localities of above threescore more priests, but that he had told him that twenty principal ones would be enough. Davies, adds Wright, will not discover the treason till he had a pardon for it himself, and on this Father Gerard remarks 'that the treason in question was none other than the Gunpowder Plot there can be no question; unless, indeed, we are to say that the authorities were engaged in fabricating a bogus conspiracy for which there was no foundation whatever in fact.' Why this inference should be drawn I do not know. If Davies was a renegade priest he would require a pardon, and in order to get it he may very

[1] Father Gerard gives the date of Davies's pardon from the Pardon Roll as April 25, 1605. It should be April 23, 1604.

well have told a story about a treason which the authorities, on further inquiry, thought it needless to investigate further. It is to no purpose that Father Gerard produces an application to James in which it is stated that Wright had furnished information to Popham and Challoner who 'had a hand in the discovery of the practices of the Jesuits in the powder plot, and did reveal the same from time to time to your Majesty, for two years' space almost before the said treason burst forth.'[1] That Wright, being in want of money, made the most of his little services in spying upon Jesuits is likely enough; but if he had come upon Gunpowder Plot two years before the Monteagle letter, that is to say, in October, 1603, some five months before it was in existence, except, perhaps, in Catesby's brain, we may be certain that he would have been far more specific in making his claim. The same may be said of Wright's letter to Salisbury on March 26, 1606, in which he pleads for assistance 'forasmuch as his Majesty is already informed of me that in something I have been, and that hereafter I may be, a deserving man of his Majesty and the State in discovering of villainous practices.' Very gentle bleating

[1] *Gerard*, 94, 95, 254. Father Gerard ascribes this application to 'a later date' than March 1606. It was, in fact a good deal later, as the endorsement 'Mr. Secretary Conway' shows that it was not earlier than 1623. The further endorsement 'touching Wright and his services performed in the damnable plot of the Powder Treason,' proves nothing. What did Conway's clerk know beyond the contents of the application itself?

indeed for a man who had found out the Gunpowder Plot, as I have just said, before it was in existence!

Nor is much more to be made of the remainder of Father Gerard's evidence on this head. The world being what it was, what else could be expected but that there should be talk amongst priests of possible risings—Sir Everard Digby in his letter predicted as much—or even that some less wise of their number should discuss half formed plans, or that renegade priests should pick up their reckless words and report them to the Government, probably with some additions of their own? [1] When Father Gerard says that a vague statement by an informer, made as early as April 1604, refers to the Gunpowder Plot, because Coke said two years later that it did,[2] he merely shows that he has little acquaintance with the peculiar intellect of that idol of the lawyers of the day. If Father Gerard had studied, as I have had occasion to do, Coke's treatment of the case of the Earl and Countess of Somerset, he would,

[1] Father Gerard (p. 98) tells us of one Thomas Coe, who wrote on Dec. 20, 1605, telling him that he had forwarded to the King 'the primary intelligence of these late treasons.' If this claim was justified, why do we not find Coe's name, either amongst the State Papers or on the Patent Rolls, as recipient of some favour from the Crown? A still more indefensible argument of Father Gerard's is one in which a letter written to Sir Everard Digby about an otter hunt is held (p. 103) to show the existence of Government espionage, because though written before Digby was acquainted with the plot it is endorsed, 'Letter written to Sir Everard Digby—Powder Treason.' Any letter in Digby's possession would be likely to be endorsed in this way whatever its contents might have been.

[2] *Gerard*, pp. 95, 96.

I fancy, have come to the conclusion that whenever Coke smelt a mystery, there was a strong probability that it either never existed at all, or, at all events, was something very different from what Coke imagined it to be.

That the Government believed, with or without foundation, that there were plots abroad, and that priests had their full share in them, may be accepted as highly probable. It must, however, be remembered that in Salisbury's eyes merely to be a priest was *ipso facto* to be engaged in a huge conspiracy, because to convert an Englishman to the Roman Catholic faith, or to confirm him in it, was to pervert him from his due allegiance to the Crown. Regarded from this point of view, the words addressed by Salisbury to Edmondes on October 17, 1605, 'more than a week,' as Father Gerard says, 'before the first hint of danger is said to have been breathed,'[1] are seen to be perfectly in character, without imagining that the writer had any special information on the Gunpowder Plot, or any intention of making use of it to pave the way for more persecuting legislation than already existed.

"I have received" writes Salisbury, "a letter of yours . . . to which there needeth no great answer for the present . . . because I have imparted to you some part of my conceit concerning the insolencies of the priests and Jesuits, whose mouths we cannot stop better than by contemning their vain and malicious discourses, only the evil which biteth is the poisoned bait, wherewith every

[1] *Gerard*, p. 106.

youth is taken that cometh among them, which liberty (as I wrote before) must for one cause or other be retrenched." [1]

This language appears to Father Gerard to be ominous of further persecution. To me it appears to be merely ominous of an intention to refuse passports to young men of uncertain religion wishing to travel on the Continent.

We can now understand why it was that Salisbury and the Government in general were so anxious to bring home the plot, after its discovery, to some, at least, of the priests, and more especially to the Jesuits.

Three of these, Garnet, Greenway and Gerard, were in England while the plot was being devised, and were charged with complicity in it. Of the three, Garnet, the Provincial of England, was tried and executed; the other two escaped to the Continent. My own opinion is that Gerard was innocent of any knowledge of the plot,[2] and, as far as I am concerned, it is only the conduct of Garnet and Greenway that is under discussion. That they both had detailed knowledge of the plot is beyond doubt, as it stands on Garnet's own admission that he had been informed of it by Greenway, and that Greenway had heard it in confession from Catesby.[3] A great deal of ink has been spilled on the question whether Garnet ought to have revealed matters involving destruction of life which had come to his knowledge

[1] Salisbury to Edmondes, Oct. 17,1605.—*Stowe MSS.* 168, fol. 181.
[2] See *History of England,* 1603–1642, i. 238, 243.
[3] Garnet's Declaration,March 9,1606.—*Hist.Rev.* July, 1888,p.513.

in confession; but on this I do not propose to touch. It is enough here to say that the law of England takes no note of the excuse of confession, and that no blame would have been due on this score either to the Government which ordered Garnet's prosecution, or to the judges and the jury by whom he was condemned, even if there had not been evidence of his knowledge when no question of confession was involved.

In considering Garnet's case the first point to be discussed is, whether the Government tampered with the evidence against the priests, either by omitting that which made in favour of the prisoner, or by forging evidence which made against him. An instance of omission is found in the mark 'hucusque' made by Coke in the margin of Fawkes's examination of November 9, implying the rejection of his statement that, though he had received the communion at Gerard's hands as a confirmation of his oath, Gerard had not known anything of the object which had led him to communicate.[1] The practice of omitting inconvenient evidence was unfortunately common enough in those days, and all that can be said for Coke on this particular occasion is, that the examination contained many obvious falsehoods, and Coke may have thought that he was keeping back only one falsehood more. Coke, however, at Garnet's trial did not content himself with omitting the important passage, but added the statement that 'Gerard the Jesuit, being well acquainted with all designs and purposes, did give

[1] Father Gerard gives a facsimile, p. 199.

them the oath of secrecy and a mass, and they received the sacrament together at his hands.'[1] Clearly, therefore, Coke is convicted, not merely of concealing evidence making in the favour of an accused, though absent, person, but of substituting for it his own conviction without producing evidence to support it. All that can be said is, in the first place, that Gerard was not on trial, and could not therefore be affected by anything that Coke might say; and that, in the second place, even if Coke's words were—as they doubtless were—accepted by the jury, the position of the prisoners actually at the bar would be neither better nor worse.

Much more serious is Father Gerard's argument that the confession of Bates, Catesby's servant, to the effect that he had not only informed Greenway of the plot, but that Greenway had expressed approval of it, was either not genuine, or, at least, had been tampered with by the Government. As Father Gerard again italicises,[2] not a passage from the examination itself, but his own abstract of the passage, it is better to give in full so much of the assailed examination as bears upon the matter:—

"Examination of Thomas Bate,[3] servant to Robert Catesby, the 4th of December, 1605, before the Lords Commissioners.

"He confesseth that about this time twelvemonth his

[1] *Harl. MSS.* 360, fol. 112 b. [2] See p. 128.

[3] As in the case of the merchant who refused to pay the imposition on currants, 'Bate' and 'Bates' were considered interchangeable.

master asked this said examinant whether he could procure him a lodging near the Parliament House. Whereupon he went to seek some such lodging and dealt with a baker that had a room joining to the Parliament House, but the baker answered that he could not spare it.

"After that some fortnight or thereabouts (as he thinketh) his master imagining, as it seemed, that this examinant suspected somewhat of that which the said Catesby went about, called him to him at Puddle Wharf in the house of one Powell (where Catesby had taken a lodging) and in the presence of Thomas Winter, asked him what he thought what business they were about, and this examinant answered that he thought they went about some dangerous business, whereupon they asked him again what he thought the business might be, and he answered that he thought they intended some dangerous matter about the Parliament House, because he had been sent to get a lodging near that House.

"Thereupon they made this examinant take an oath to be secret in the business, which being taken by him, they told him that it was true that they meant to do somewhat about the Parliament House, namely, to lay powder under it to blow it up.

"Then they told him that he was to receive the sacrament for the more assurance, and he thereupon went to confession to a priest named Greenway, and in his confession told Greenway that he was to conceal a very dangerous piece of work that his master Catesby and Thomas Winter had imparted unto him, and that he being fearful of it, asked the counsel of Greenway, telling the said Greenway (which he was not desirous to hear) their particular intent and purpose of blowing up the Parliament House, and Greenway the priest thereto said that he would take no notice thereof, but that he, the said examinant, should be secret in that which his master had imparted unto him, because that was for a good cause, and that he willed this examinant to tell no other priest of it; saying moreover that it was not dangerous unto him nor any offence to conceal it, and thereupon the said priest Greenway gave this examinant absolution, and he received the sacrament in the company of his master Robert Catesby and Mr. Thomas Winter.

. . . . .

"Thomas Bate,
Nottingham,
Suffolk,
E. Worcester,

H. Northampton,
Salisbury,
Mar,
Dunbar."

Indorsed :—"*The exam.* of Tho. Bate 4 Dec. 1605. *Greenway*, §."[1]

Out of this document arise two questions which ought to be kept carefully distinct:—

1. Did the Government invent or falsify the document here partially printed?
2. Did Bates, on the hypothesis that the document is genuine, tell the truth about Greenway?

1. In the first place, Father Gerard calls our attention to the fact that the document has only reached us in a copy. It is quite true; though, on the other hand, I must reiterate the argument, which I have already used in a similar case,[2] that a copy in which the names of the Commissioners appear, even though not under their own hands, falls not far short of an original. If this copy, being a forgery, were read in court, as Father

[1] *G. P. B.*, No. 145. The words in italics are added in a different hand. Dunbar's name does not occur in the list of Commissioners at p. 24.

[2] See p. 41.

Gerard says it was,[1] some of the Commissioners would have felt aggrieved at their names being misused, unless, indeed, the whole seven concurred in authorising the forgery, which is so extravagant a supposition that we are bound to look narrowly into any evidence brought forward to support it.

Father Gerard's main argument in favour of the conclusion at which he leads up to—one can hardly say he arrives at this or any other clearly announced conviction—is put in the following words:—

> "If, however, this version were not genuine, but prepared for a purpose, it is clear that it could not have been produced while Bates was alive to contradict it, and there appears to be no doubt that it was not heard of till after his death."

The meaning of this is, that the Government did not dare to produce the confession till after Bates's death, lest he should contradict it. If this were true it would no doubt furnish a strong argument against the genuineness of the confession, though not a conclusive one, because at the trial of that batch of the prisoners among whom Bates stood, the Government may have wished to reserve the evidence to be used against Greenway, whom it chiefly concerned, if they still hoped to catch him. I do not, however, wish to insist on this suggestion, as I hope to be able to show that

[1] *Gerard*, p. 179. I do not think his argument on this point conclusive, but obviously it would be useless to forge a document unless it was to be used in evidence.

the evidence was produced at Bates's trial, when he had the opportunity, if he pleased, of replying to it.

Father Gerard's first argument is, that in a certain 'manuscript account of the plot,[1] written between the trial of the conspirators and that of Garnet, that is, within two months of the former,' the author, though he argues that the priests must have been cognizant of the design, says nothing of the case of Bates's evidence against Greenway, 'but asserts him to have been guilty only because his Majesty's proclamation so speaks it.'[2] To this it may be answered that, in the first place, the manuscript does not profess to be a history of the plot. It contains the story of the arrest of Garnet and other persons, and is followed by the story of the taking of Robert Winter and Stephen Littleton. In the second place, there is strong reason to suppose, not only from the subjects chosen by the writer, but also from his mode of treating them, that he was not only a Stafford-shire man, or an inhabitant of some county near Wolverhampton, but that his narrative was drawn up at no great distance from Wolverhampton. It does not follow that because his Majesty's proclamation had been heard of in Wolverhampton, a piece of evidence produced in court at Westminster would have reached so far.

Another argument used by Father Gerard in his own favour, appears to me to tell against him. In a copy of a minute of Salisbury's to a certain Favat,

[1] *Harl. MSS.* 360, fol. 96. [2] *Gerard*, p 170.

who had been employed by the King to write to him, we find the following statement, which undoubtedly refers to Bates's confession, it being written on December 4, the day on which it was taken :—

"You may tell his Majesty that if he please to read privately what this day we have drawn from a voluntary and penitent examination, the point I am persuaded (but I am no undertaker) shall be so well cleared, if he forebear to speak much of this but ten days, as he shall see all fall out to that end whereat his Majesty shooteth." [1]

Father Gerard's comment on this, that the confession of Bates, here referred to, 'cannot be that afterwards given to the world; for it is spoken of as affording promise, but not yet satisfactory in its performance.' [2] Yes; but promise of what? The King, it may be presumed, had asked not merely to know what Greenway had done, but to know what had been the conduct of all the priests who had confessed the plotters. The early part of the minute is clear upon that. Salisbury writes that the King wanted

'to learn the names of those priests which have been confessors and ministers of the sacrament to those conspirators, because it followeth indeed in consequence that they could not be ignorant of their purposes, seeing all men that doubt resort to them for satisfaction, and all men use confession to obtain absolution.'

Bearing this in mind, and also that Salisbury goes

[1] Salisbury's Minute to Favat, Dec. 4, 1605.—*Add. MSS.* 6178, fol. 98.

[2] *Gerard*, p. 181.

on to say that 'most of the conspirators have carefully forsworn that the priests knew anything particular, and obstinately refused to be accusers of them, yea what torture soever they be put to,' I cannot see that anything short of the statement about Greenway ascribed to Bates would justify Salisbury's satisfaction with what he had learnt, though he qualifies his pleasure with the thought that there is much more still to be learnt about Greenway himself, as well as about other priests. An autograph postscript to a letter written to Edmondes on March 8, 1606, shows Salisbury in exactly the spirit which I have here ascribed to him :—

"You may now confidently affirm that Whalley[1] is guilty *ex ore proprio*. This day confessed of the Gunpowder Treason, but he saith he devised it not, only he concealed it when Father Greenway *alias* Tesmond did impart to him all particulars, and Catesby only the general. Thus do you see that Greenway is now by the superintendent as guilty as we have accused him. He confesseth also that Greenway told him that Father Owen was privy to all. More will now come after this."[2]

The tone of the letter to Favat is more subdued than this, as befitted writing that was to come under the King's eye; but the meaning is identical :—"I have got much, but I hope for more."

We now come to Father Gerard's argument that

[1] An *alias* for Garnet.

[2] Salisbury to Edmondes, March 8, 1606.—*Stowe MSS.* 168, fol. 366.

the charge against Greenway of approving the plot was not produced even at Garnet's trial on March 28, 1606, Bates having been tried on January 27, and being executed on the 30th :—

"Still more explicit is the evidence furnished by another MS. containing a report of Father Garnet's trial. In this the confession of Bates is cited, but precisely the significant passage of which we have spoken, as follows: 'Catesby afterwards discovered the project unto him; shortly after which discovery, Bates went to mass to Tesimond [Greenway] and there was confessed and had absolution.'

"Here, again, it is impossible to suppose that the all-important point was the one omitted. It is clear, however, that the mention of a confession made to Greenway would *primâ facie* afford a presumption that this particular matter had been confessed, thus furnishing a foundation whereon to build; and knowing, as we do, how evidence was manipulated, it is quite conceivable that the copy now extant incorporates the improved version thus suggested."

Father Gerard has quoted the sentence about Bates and Greenway correctly,[1] but he has not observed that Coke, in his opening speech, is stated on the same authority to have expressed himself as follows :—

"In November following comes Bates to Greenway the Jesuit, and tells him all his master's purpose; he hears his confession, absolves him, and encourageth him to go on, saying it is for the good of the Catholic cause, and therefore warrantable."[2]

I acknowledge that Coke's unsupported assertion is

[1] *Harl. MSS.* 360, fol. 117. [2] *Ib.* fol. 113.

worth very little; but I submit that so practised an advocate would hardly have produced a confession which, if it contained no more than Father Gerard supposes, would have directly refuted his own statement. Father Gerard, I fancy, fails to take into account the difficulties of note-takers in days prior to the invention of shorthand. The report-taker had followed the early part of Bates's examination fairly well. Then come the words quoted by Father Gerard at the very bottom of the page. May not the desire to get all that he had to say into that page have been too strong for the reporter, especially as, after what Coke had said earlier in the day, the statement that Bates 'confessed' might reasonably be supposed to cover the subject of confession? 'Catesby . . . discovered the project unto him, shortly after which discovery' he confessed. What can he be supposed to have confessed except the project discovered? and, if so, Greenway's absolution implies approval.

Father Gerard, moreover, though he quotes from another manuscript Garnet's objection that 'Bates was a dead man,' thereby meaning that Bates's testimony was now worthless, entirely omits to notice that the preceding paragraph is destructive of his contention. A question had arisen as to whether Greenway had shown contrition.

"Nay," replied Mr. Attorney, "I am sure that he had not, for to Bates he approved the fact, and said he had no obligation to reveal it to any other ghostly father, to which effect Bates his confession was produced, which verified as much as Mr. Attorney said, and then Mr. Attorney added that he had heard by men more learned than he, that if for defect of contrition it was not a sacrament, then it might lawfully be revealed.

"Mr. Garnet rejoined that Bates was a dead man, and therefore although he would not discredit him, yet he was bound to keep that secret which was spoken in confession as well as Greenway."[1]

Having thus shown that Father Gerard's argument, that the statement about Greenway was not produced at Garnet's trial, cannot be maintained; that his argument drawn from the account of the arrest of Garnet and others is irrelevant, and that Salisbury's letter to Favat, so far from contradicting the received story, goes a long way to confirm it, I proceed to ask why we are not to accept the report of *A true and perfect relation*, where Coke is represented as giving the substance of the confession of Bates, beginning with Catesby's revelation of the plot to him, followed by his full confession to Greenway and Greenway's answer, somewhat amplified indeed, as Coke's manner was, but obviously founded on Bates's confession of December 4, 1605.

"Then they," *i.e.* Catesby and Winter, "told him that he was to receive the sacrament for the more assurance, and thereupon he went to confession to the said Tesmond the Jesuit, and in his confession told him that he was to conceal a very dangerous piece of work, that his master

[1] *Add. MSS.* 21203, fol. 38 b.

Catesby and Thomas Winter had imparted unto him, and said he much feared the matter to be utterly unlawful, and therefore thereon desired the counsel of the Jesuit, and revealed unto him the whole intent and purpose of blowing up the Parliament House upon the first day of the assembly, at what time the King, the Queen, the Prince, the Lords spiritual and temporal, the judges, knights, citizens, burgesses should all have been there convented and met together. But the Jesuit being a confederate therein before, resolved and encouraged him in the action, and said that he should be secret in that which his master had imparted unto him, for that it was for a good cause, adding, moreover, that it was not dangerous unto him nor any offence to conceal it; and thereupon the Jesuit gave him absolution, and Bates received the sacrament of him, in the company of his master, Robert Catesby, and Thomas Winter."[1]

We have not, indeed, the evidence set forth, but we have a distinct intimation that amongst the confessions read was one from which 'it appeared that Bates was resolved from what he understood concerning the powder treason, and being therein warranted by the Jesuits.'[2]

2. Being now able to assume that the confession ascribed to Bates was genuine, the further question arises whether Bates told the truth or not. We have, in the first place, Greenway's strong protestation that he had not heard of the plot from Bates. In the second place, Father Gerard adduces a retractation by

[1] *A true and perfect relation.* Sig. G., 2, *verso.*

[2] *Ib.*, Sig. K., 3.

Bates of a statement that he thought Greenway 'knew of the business.' Now, whatever inference we choose to draw, it is a curious fact that this has nothing to do with Bates's confession of December 4—the letter of Bates printed in the narrative of the Gerard who lived in the seventeenth century running as follows:—

"At my last being before them I told them I thought Greenway knew of this business, but I did not charge the others with it, but that I saw them all together with my master at my Lord Vaux's, and that after I saw Mr. Whalley," *i.e.* Garnet, "and Mr. Greenway at Coughton, and it is true. For I was sent thither with a letter, and Mr. Greenway rode with me to Mr. Winter's to my master, and from thence he rode to Mr. Abington's. This I told them, and no more. For which I am heartily sorry for, and I trust God will forgive me, for I did it not out of malice but in hope to gain my life by it, which I think now did me no good." [1]

This clearly refers not to the confession of December 4, but to that of January 13, in which these matters were spoken of, and it is to be noted that Bates does not acknowledge having spoken falsely, but of having told inconvenient truths.

Bates's entire silence in this letter as to the confession of December 4 may receive one of two interpretations. Either Greenway was not mentioned in that confession at all—a solution which in the face of

[1] Morris's *Condition of Catholics*, 210. A Latin translation of part of the letter was printed in 1610, by Eudæmon Joannes, *Ad actionem proditoriam, &c.*, p. 6.

[2] *G. P. B.*, No. 166.

Salisbury's letter to Favat seems to be an impossible one—or else Bates knew that he had at that time made disclosures to which he did not wish to refer. It is, perhaps, not so very unlikely that he compounded for what would in any case be regarded as a great fault by disclosing a smaller one.

Are we, then, shut up to the conclusion that Father Greenway sheltered himself by telling a deliberate lie? I do not see that it is absolutely necessary; though I suppose, under correction, that he might feel himself bound to aver that he had never heard what he had only heard in confession. Is it not, however, possible that Bates in confessing to Greenway did not go into the details of the plot, but merely spoke of some design against the Government with which his master had entrusted him, and that Greenway told him that it was his master's secret, and he might be content to think that it was in a good cause?[1] As time went on Bates would easily read his own knowledge of the plot into the words he had used in confession, or may even have deliberately expanded his statement to please the examiners. Life was dear, and he may have hoped to gain pardon if he could throw the blame on a Jesuit. Besides, Greenway, as he probably knew, had not been arrested, and no harm would come if he painted him blacker than he was. This is but a conjecture, but if it is anywhere near the mark, it is easy to understand why Bates should not have been eager to call attention to the confession of

[1] See the express words ascribed to Bates at p. 180.

December 4, when he wrote the letter which has been already quoted.[1] On the other hand Catesby seems to have had no doubt of Greenway's adherence, as is shown by his exclaiming on the priest's arrival at Coughton, that 'here, at least, was a gentleman that would live and die with them.'

In any case, the general attitude of the priests is not difficult to imagine. Not even their warmest advocates can suppose that they received the news of a plot to blow up James I. and his Parliament with quite as much abhorrence as they would have manifested if they had heard of a plot to blow up the Pope and the College of Cardinals. They were men who had suffered much and were exposed at any moment to suffer more. They held that James had broken his promise without excuse. But they had their instructions from Rome to discountenance all disturbances; and we may do them the justice to add that both Garnet and Greenway were shocked when they were informed of the atrocious character of the plot itself; but, at all events, Sir Everard Digby was able to write from prison to his wife:—

"Before that I knew anything of the plot, I did ask Mr. Farmer," *i.e.* Garnet, "what the meaning of the Pope's Brief was; he told me that they were not (meaning priests) to undertake or procure stirs; but yet they would not hinder any, neither was it the Pope's mind they should, that should be undertaken for the Catholic good. I did never utter thus much, nor would not but to you; and this

[1] See p. 190.

answer with Mr. Catesby's proceedings with him and me give me absolute belief that the matter in general was approved, though every particular was not known."[1]

Whatever may be thought of the value of this statement Garnet's attitude towards the plot was, on his own showing, hardly one of unqualified abhorrence. Assuming that all that Greenway had informed him of on one particular occasion, when the whole design was poured into his ears, was told under the sanction of the confessional, and that not only the rule of his Church, but other more worldly considerations, prohibited the disclosure of anything so heard, there was all the more reason why he should take any opportunity that occurred to learn the secret out of confession, and so to do his utmost to prevent the atrocious design from being carried into execution. Let us see whether he did so or not, on his own showing.

On June 8 or 9, 1605,[2] Catesby asked Garnet the question whether it was lawful to kill innocent persons, together with nocents, on the pretence that his inquiry related to the siege of a town in war. At first Garnet treated the question as of no other import. "I . . . thought it at the first but as it were an idle question, till I saw him, when we had done, make solemn protesta-

[1] Sir E. Digby's Papers, No. 9, published at the end of Bishop Barlow's reprint of *The Gunpowder Treason*.

[2] The Saturday or Sunday after the octave of Corpus Christi, *i.e.*, June 8 or 9, old style, which seems to have been used, as the same day is described as being about the beginning of Trinity Term, which began on May 31.

tion that he would never be known to have asked me any such question so long as he lived." On this Garnet began to muse within himself as to Catesby's meaning.

"And," he continues, "fearing lest he should intend the death of some great persons, and by seeking to draw them together enwrap not only innocents but friends and necessary persons for the Commonwealth, I thought I would take fit occassion to admonish him that upon my speech he should not run headlong to so great a mischief."

Garnet accordingly talked to him when he met him next, towards the end of June, telling him that he wished him 'to look what he did if he intended anything, that he must not have so little regard of innocents that he spare not friends and necessary persons to a Commonwealth, and told him what charge we had of all quietness, and to procure the like of others.' It was certainly rather mild condemnation of a design which, as Garnet understood, would involve considerable loss of life.

Soon afterwards Garnet received a letter from the General of the Society, directing him, in the Pope's name, to hinder all conspiracies, and this letter he showed to Catesby when next he saw him:—

"I showed him my letter from Rome," wrote Garnet afterwards, "and admonished him of the Pope's pleasure. I doubted he had some device in his head, whatsoever it was, being against the Pope's will, it could not prosper. He said that what he meant to do, if the Pope knew, he would not hinder, for the general good of the country. But I being earnest with him, and inculcating the Pope's prohibition did add this *quia expresse hoc Papa non vult et prohibet,* he told me he was not bound to take knowledge by me of the Pope's will. I said indeed my own credit was but little, but our General, whose letter I had read to him, was a man everywhere respected for his wisdom and virtue, so I desired him that before he attempted anything he would acquaint the Pope. He said he would not for all the world make his particular project known to him, for fear of discovery. I wished him at the last in general to inform him how things stood here by some lay gentleman."

This suggestion took shape in the mission of Sir Edmund Baynham. We are only concerned here with Garnet's expostulations, and again it must be said that they appear to have been singularly mild, considering all that Catesby had admitted.

A few days later Garnet learnt the whole truth from Greenway, in a way which is said to have been tantamount to confession. Admitting once more that he may have been bound to keep silence to others on these details, he could not keep silence to himself. There are no partitions in the brain to divide what one wishes to know from what one wishes not to know, and if Garnet thoroughly abhorred the plot, he was surely bound to take up Catesby's earlier self-revelations, and to strive to the uttermost to probe the matter to the bottom, in all legitimate ways. No doubt he had moments in which his conscience was sorely troubled, but they were followed by no decisive action, and it is useless to say that he expected to meet Catesby at 'All-hallow-tide.' With all the Jesuit machinery under his hands, he could surely have found Catesby out between July and November, and this omission is perhaps the most fatal condemnation of Garnet's course. If he had for many months known enough otherwise than in confession to enable him to remonstrate with Catesby in November, why could he not have remonstrated four months before with much more hope of success?

Still more serious is Garnet's own account of his feelings when Greenway imparted the story to him, saying that he thought the plot unlawful, and 'a most horrible thing.' He charged Greenway 'to hinder it if he could, for he knew well enough what strict prohibition we had had.' Greenway replied 'that in truth he had disclaimed it, and protested that he did not approve it, and that he would do what lay in him to dissuade it.' Yet up to the discovery of the plot, Garnet, though he met Greenway at least once, took no means of inquiring how Greenway had fared in his enterprise. "How he performed it after," he explained, "I have not heard but by the report of Bates's confession." [1]

On July 24, Garnet writes a letter to the General of his Society, in which, as we are told, nothing learnt only in confession ought to have been introduced. Accordingly, either in this or a later letter,[2] he merely speaks

[1] Garnet's Declaration, March 9.—*Hist. Rev.*, July 1888 pp. 510–517

[2] The letter is printed in Tierney's *Dodd*, iv. App. cix., where there is an argument in a note to show that the part from which I am about to quote came from a later letter. For my purpose the date is immaterial.

in general terms of the danger of any private treason or violence against the King, and asks for the orders of his Holiness as to what is to be done in the case, and a formal prohibition of the use of armed force. Surely some stronger language would be expected here. It is true that, according to his own account, Garnet remained 'in great perplexity,' and prayed that God 'would dispose of all for the best, and find the best means which were pleasing to Him to prevent so great a mischief.' He tells us, indeed, that he wrote constantly to Rome 'to get a prohibition under censures of all attempts,' but as the answer he got was that the Pope was of the opinion that 'his general prohibition would serve,' it does not seem likely that Garnet enlarged on the real danger more than he had done in the letter referred to above. He expected, he says, some further action; 'and that hope and Mr. Catesby's promise of doing nothing until Sir Edmund had been with the Pope made me think that either nothing would be done or not before the end of the Parliament; before what time we should surely hear, as undoubtedly we should if Baynham had gone to Rome as soon as I imagined.'[1] In a further declaration, Garnet disclosed that there was more in his conduct than misplaced hopefulness. Speaking of Catesby's first consultation with himself, he adds :—

"Neither ever did I enter further with him then, as I

[1] Garnet's Declaration, March 9.—*Hist. Rev.*, July 1888, pp. 510–517.

wrote, but rather cut off all occasions (after I knew his project) of any discoursing with him of it, thereby to save myself harmless both with the state here, and with my superiors at Rome, to whom I knew this thing would be infinitely displeasing, insomuch as at my second conference with Mr. Greenwell," *i.e.* Greenway, "I said 'Good Lord, if this matter go forward, the Pope will send me to the galleys, for he will assuredly think I was privy to it.'"[1]

To say that Garnet had two consciences, an official and a personal one, would doubtless err by giving too brutally clear-cut a definition of the mysterious workings of the mind. Yet we shall probably be right in thinking not only that, as a Catholic, a priest, and a Jesuit, he was bound to carry out the directions conveyed to him from the Pope, but that those directions commended themselves to his own mind whenever he set himself seriously to consider the matter. It was but human weakness[2] to be so shocked by the persecution going on around him as to regard with some complacency the horrors which sought to put a stop to it, or at least to find excuses for omitting to inquire, where inquiry must necessarily lead to active resistance. The Government theory that Garnet and the other Jesuits had originated the plot

[1] Garnet's Declaration, March 10.—*Hist. Rev.*, July 1888, p. 517.

[2] The author of Sir Everard Digby's life writes:—"I fully admit that if Father Garnet was weak, his weakness was owing to an excess of kindheartedness and a loyalty to his friends that bordered on extravagance." (*The Life of a Conspirator*, by 'One of his Descendants,' p. 134.) It will be noticed that I am inclined to go further than this.

was undoubtedly false, but, as far as we are able to judge, they did not look upon it with extraordinary horror, neither did they take such means as were lawful and possible to avert the disaster.

To sum up the conclusions to which I have been led. There may be difference of opinion as to my suggested explanations of some details in the 'traditional' story; but as a whole it stands untouched by Father Gerard's criticisms. What is more, no explanation has been offered by any one which will fit in with the evidence which I have adduced in its favour. As for the plot itself, it was the work of men indignant at the banishment of the priests after the promises made by James in Scotland. The worse persecution which followed no doubt sharpened their indignation and led to the lukewarmness with which Garnet opposed it; but it had nothing to do with the inception of the plot.

As to the action of the Government, it was in the main straightforward. It had to disguise its knowledge that James did not discover the plot by Divine inspiration, and having firmly persuaded itself that the Jesuits had been at the bottom of the whole affair, it suppressed at least one statement to the contrary, which it may very well have believed to be untrue, whilst the Attorney General—not a man easily restrained—put forward his own impression as positive truth, though he had no evidence behind it. On the other hand, James, having before him in writing

Garnet's account of the information gained from Greenway in confession, refused to allow it to be used against the prisoner.

The attempt to make Salisbury the originator of the Plot for his own purposes breaks down entirely, if only because, at the time when the plot was started, he had already pushed James to take the first step in the direction in which he wished him to go, and that every succeeding step carried him further in the same direction. It is also highly probable that he had no information about it till the Monteagle letter was placed in his hands. That there was a plot at all is undoubtedly owing to James's conduct in receding from his promises. Yet, even his fault in this respect raises more difficult questions than Roman Catholic writers are inclined to admit. The question of toleration was a new one, and James may be credited with a sincere desire to avoid persecution for religion. He was, however, confronted by the question of allegiance. If the Roman Catholics increased in numbers, so far as to become a power in the land, would they or the Pope tolerate a 'heretic' King? This was the real crux of the situation. In the nineteenth century it is not felt, and we can regard it lightly. In the beginning of the seventeenth century men could remember how Henry IV. had been driven to submit to the Papal Church on pain of exclusion from the throne. Was there ever to be a possibility of the like happening to James? There can be no doubt that he believed in the doctrines of his own Church as firmly as any Jesuit believed in those which it was his duty to maintain. But, though this question of doctrine must not be left out of sight, it must by no means be forced into undue prominence. It was the question of allegiance that was at stake. James tried hard to avoid it, and it must be acknowledged that his efforts were, to some extent, reciprocated from the other side,[1] but the gulf could not be bridged over. In the end the antagonism took its fiercest shape in the disputation on the new oath of allegiance enjoined on all recusants in 1606. The respective claims of Pope and King to divine right were then brought sharply into collision. Now that we are removed by nearly three centuries from the combatants, we may look somewhat beyond the contentions of the disputants. Behind the arguments of the Royalist, we may discern the claim of a nation for supreme control over its own legislation and government. Behind the arguments of the Papalist, we may discern an anxiety to forbid any chance occupant of a throne, or any chance parliamentary majority, from dictating to the consciences of those who in all temporal matters are ready to yield obedience to existing authority.

[1] In addition to what has been already said, a letter from the Nuncio at Brussels to Dr. Gifford, written on $\frac{\text{July 22}}{\text{Aug. 1}}$, 1604, may be quoted. He says that the Pope 'paratissimum esse ea omnia pro suâ in Catholicos authoritate facere quæ Serenissimæ suæ Majestati securitatem suæ personæ et status procurare possunt, eosque omnes e regno evocare quos sua Majestas rationabiliter judicaverit regno et statui [MS. statuti] suo noxios fore.'—*Tierney's Dodd*, App. No. 5.

INDEX